christinemanfield originals

Christine Manfield Originals is the long-awaited paperback edition of the bestselling *Paramount Cooking*.

Christine Manfield is one of Australia's most celebrated chefs – a perfectionist inspired by strong flavours, and a writer whose other successful books, *Spice*, *Stir* and *Christine Manfield Desserts*, have encouraged keen cooks from Melbourne to Manchester to Manhattan.

After working with some of Australia's best restaurateurs, in 1993 Christine opened the Paramount Restaurant in Sydney, and the groundbreaking Paramount Store three doors away. Paramount was regarded as one of the finest in Australia by critics and the dining public alike. Since its closure at the end of 2000, Christine has broadened her global food interests, working alongside respected chefs around the world and hosting gastronomic tours to exotic destinations including Morocco, India, Spain and Turkey. As an ongoing legacy of her prepared food products at the Store, Christine developed her signature Spice Collection, a range of pastes and condiments that are available across Australia and at selected stores overseas.

Christine surrendered to a niggling restlessness when she was approached to create a new restaurant and lounge bar in London's West End. East@West opened in late 2003, introducing Londoners to the unique kaleidoscope of tastes and refined textures with her signature Modern Asian-inspired menus. The restaurant closed in early 2005 when sold by its owners but not before winning several awards, including Tatler's Best New Restaurant, Best UK Menu at the Catey's Awards, three rosettes at the AA Restaurant Awards, and runner-up for the Best Vegetarian Menu at the Time Out Restaurant Awards. Christine continues her portfolio of work projects in Australia and overseas.

christinemanfield originals

photography by ashley barber

LANTERN
an imprint of
PENGUIN BOOKS

LANTERN

Published by the Penguin Group
Penguin Group (Australia)
250 Camberwell Road, Camberwell, Victoria 3124, Australia
(a division of Pearson Australia Group Pty Ltd)
Penguin Group (USA) Inc.
375 Hudson Street, New York, New York 10014, USA
Penguin Group (Canada)
90 Eglinton Avenue East, Suite 700, Toronto ON M4P 2Y3, Canada
(a division of Pearson Penguin Canada Inc.)
Penguin Books Ltd
80 Strand, London WC2R 0RL, England
Penguin Ireland
25 St Stephen's Green, Dublin 2, Ireland
(a division of Penguin Books Ltd)
Penguin Books India Pvt Ltd
11 Community Centre, Panchsheel Park, New Delhi – 110 017, India
Penguin Group (NZ)
Cnr Airborne and Rosedale Roads, Albany, Auckland, New Zealand
(a division of Pearson New Zealand Ltd)
Penguin Books (South Africa) (Pty) Ltd
24 Sturdee Avenue, Rosebank, Johannesburg 2196, South Africa

Penguin Books Ltd, Registered Offices: 80 Strand, London WC2R 0RL, England

First published as *Paramount Cooking* by Penguin Books Australia Ltd, 1995
This edition, *Christine Manfield Originals*, published by Penguin Group (Australia),
a division of Pearson Australia Group Pty Ltd, 2006

10 9 8 7 6 5 4 3 2 1

Cover design by Patrick Leong © Penguin Group (Australia)
Text design by Guy Mirabella © Penguin Group (Australia)
Photography by Ashley Barber
Restaurant and Store photos by Sharrin Rees
Typeset in Garamond and Frutiger by Bookset, Melbourne
Printed and bound in China by 1010 Printing International Limited

National Library of Australia
Cataloguing-in-Publication data:

Manfield, Christine.
Christine Manfield Originals.

Includes index.
ISBN 1 920989 46 3.

1. Cookery, Australian. I. Title.

641.5994

www.penguin.com.au

Front cover photograph: Wok-seared tuna and tatsoi with lemongrass, chilli, basil and roasted peanuts (see page 44)

Back cover photograph: Blue swimmer crab, shaved coconut and mint salad with fried shallots (see page 56)

Contents

This book is a tribute to my partner, Margie Harris, who has been part of the vision from the beginning and has given me her unquestioned support and devotion to an ideal. She is my greatest critic and my greatest fan and has made the entire process memorable, possible and endurable.

Introduction

MY PHILOSOPHY of life and work is based on the premise that life is too short to eat bad food. I am motivated by passion, care and integrity, not by profit at the expense of those qualities. My driving ambition has always been the pursuit of excellence and that is what guides me in my work and my life. Attention to detail is of utmost importance. Mediocrity has no place in my world; it smacks of sloppiness, slackness, indifference and many weaknesses. Strength of character, the ability to learn through criticism and the obsessiveness that forces me to push myself to the limits physically, mentally and emotionally affect the way I work and how I expect those around me to work. It breeds a toughness and is a quality I seek in others.

These words allow me to reflect on the time that has passed since I originally wrote them, and I find they remain as relevant and pertinent today as they did then. Nothing has changed, although I have travelled and worked far and wide since those days in the early nineties of the Paramount Restaurant and Paramount Store and their daily menus, around which this book's contents are based. If anything, I am more resolute than ever to stand apart from the pack, to remain an active player at the forefront of culinary evolution and development, to stand by this mantra. These original recipes, developed to embody the personality of Paramount, have stood the test of time and remain an important part of my working repertoire with flavours and textures that are as relevant today as they were when first introduced to the dining public.

As always, I continue to enjoy cooking for and being with people who celebrate the richness and diversity that food offers us in our daily lives, and who understand how it affects our wellbeing and its important role in the social process. People should not be afraid of food or its preparation; it is an act of generosity, it comes from the heart. I enjoy being cooked for as much as cooking for other people. Never be intimidated by the act of cooking; never fret about who you are cooking for; just relax, get on with it and find that strength and confidence within yourself – it will be expressed in your food. Great communication can happen through food: it provides a universal language that transcends all borders and is empowering to all that embrace it. After all, eating is a personal and subliminal act. It relies on many senses and experiences. What and how we eat is based on knowledge, understanding, attitude, income, availability and acceptance. Any opinion is coloured by all these facts, so pure objectivity is an illusion; the bottom line is that we must trust our own perceptions and desires. Critical analysis is an important and viable aspect of the entire eating procedure but it must be considered within these parameters.

The culture and demands of restaurant life became an all-consuming passion that began in Adelaide in 1986 after I abandoned the safe haven of a teaching career. In 1988 my personal journey led me to Sydney, where institutional learning paled into insignificance compared to the working relationships and opportunities I was fortunate enough to have in those formative years. There were and are many in the industry whom I hold in the highest regard, who command respect and provide inspiration. Our culinary world and intellectual life are all the richer for their presence. Margie Harris and I went on to operate our own business for ten years with close to eight years at Paramount before we closed its doors at the end of 2000 to pursue other goals and life experiences.

When the Paramount Restaurant opened its doors in July 1993, we realised our dream of having a space that we could call our own and the luxury of being in total control of the entire package. It proved exhilarating, exhausting, demanding, inspirational, collaborative, challenging and nerve-racking, but neither of us would have swapped that opportunity with anything at the time. Our working partnership started in 1990 when we opened dining rooms in two hotels in Sydney and had blossomed to the point that we knew we were ready to take the next big step. With the advent of Paramount Restaurant we could concentrate solely on one place – a place of our own making, where we made all the decisions and rules, which was reflected in every aspect of the restaurant. Restaurants of this nature are driven by the personality of their owners as much as the food; both feed off each other and leave an indelible mark. We controlled the cooking, the service, the wine, the attitude, the ambience – all the components that make up a restaurant – driven by the pursuit of excellence.

A mere three months after the restaurant opened we were offered the opportunity to take over a small space almost next door to the restaurant, and in our infinite madness at the time Margie and I collaborated with my then second chef, Barbara Alexander – who had a supreme working knowledge of my food and thoroughly understood and embodied my working philosophy – to take it on as her project to manage and oversee. Barbara had my implicit trust to make the vision a reality, and she took it on with relish and eternal energy. The Store was with us for eighteen months before the building was sold and pulled down to make way for new apartments. A stunning space, spare and minimal yet intriguing to the passer-by, it embodied the design principle of 'less is more', and was designed by the same team that created the restaurant: Iain Halliday and David Katon. We made everything that was sold there under the Paramount label. It was certainly ahead of its time and it took several years before others started to emulate it. We looked at the market with lateral vision and provided restaurant-quality food at the retail level, with every detail covered and considered. We wanted to expand the services of the area, because the street had a cosy, village atmosphere with an interesting make-up of residents and high-density living. We saw our position as one of enhancement, because we were also local residents.

The intention of the Store was to provide a variety of services to people who wished to cook or entertain at home. It was possible to purchase preparations that formed the basis of cooking, removing some of the time-consuming processes and allowing the cook to produce food that was interesting, packed with flavour but not factory processed. We also offered ready-made items, such as pastes, dressings, sauces, baked items, ready-to-go dinners, cakes, biscuits, breads, ice-creams and sorbets – many things of indulgence. Our ambition for the Store was to maintain

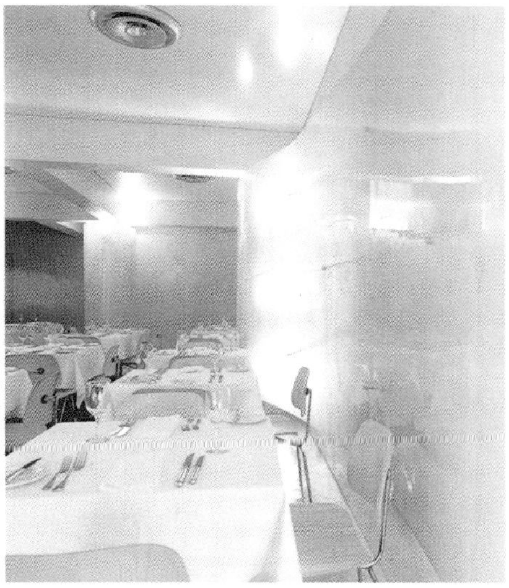

The mellow interior of the Paramount Restaurant featured a fibreglass wall

The Paramount Restaurant in Potts Point viewed from the outside

The Paramount Store viewed from the outside

total control and to limit the availability of its goods to on-site. Everything had to measure up to the same exacting standards as the Restaurant, to live up to the Paramount philosophy of providing well-crafted, elegant food with assertive flavours. As a consequence, the two establishments bore a direct relationship with each other and gave consumers greater diversity in their eating choices, habits and lifestyles. The Store became a benchmark for others to follow. I made the statement then that the future direction of food in Australia was dependent on us maintaining honesty about our produce and the ensuing processes of preparation, not succumbing to the dominance of inferior mass-produced food. This holds as true today as it did then; the battle continues to win the minds and palates of people everywhere to make considered and informed choices about what they consume.

More recently, I spent eighteen months in London opening a new Modern Asian restaurant in Covent Garden, a frenetic yet fantastic burst of energy, shortened by the sudden sale of the restaurant in early 2005 – but not before it received several awards and critical acclaim. I relished the challenges then as much as I do now and fully expect to encounter many more along this fascinating journey that I have embarked on, knowing that any number of possibilities lie in wait. Whatever happens, I will maintain a strong sense of purpose, a disciplined focus, an intensity, a thorough attention to detail and a steely determination to be successful for the right reasons. The essence of my work is to constantly redefine the boundaries and to pass on these essential skills to the people who work with me who are worthy of my time, effort and energy.

The recipes in this book reflect my love of well-crafted food with assertive flavours, a philosophy that cemented itself at Paramount and continues to play an integral role in my work today. I have included the original introductions and commentary about the recipes, because my thoughts are still relevant today. The chapters spring from some useful basic building blocks that can be prepared and stored as essential items in your pantry, making the next stage of cooking more rewarding and less time-consuming. The recipes offer an insight into how these basics can be used to create rewarding dishes that vary in complexity, so tackle first those you find achievable. Although I have provided quite precise quantities to reduce confusion and the element of error so as to make the process more accurate, I would also suggest that as you become more comfortable and confident with the recipes and their parts, you can adjust and amend where necessary. Cooking is about adaptation, refinement and change; I do not see it as an absolute.

The recipes generally serve six, but occasionally you may come across one part of a recipe that yields more. Do not worry! It is one of my foibles to err on the side of generosity. The extra dressing, sauce or paste can be kept for later use. Cooking well does demand time, patience, organisation, reading and thinking, but the subsequent sense of achievement is satisfying and unparalleled.

Christine Manfield

Sydney 2006

ACKNOWLEDGEMENTS It may be my name on the door or the book, but I would like to acknowledge all those who made Paramount Restaurant and Store what it was, the entire team that made it happen, with particular credit to those who became like family and continue to play a part in my life, my inner sanctum – chefs Barbara Alexander, Jessica Muir, Bernie Plaisted, Ian (Paddy) Atkinson, Alexandra Miller, Virginia Jones and Jarrod Hudson; Sido Bilson, Peter Hurren and Nigel Nickless, the stars of the floor who started at the beginning and helped us close the doors when the party was over; and to all those who helped us celebrate our closing with *The Last Dance* – a farewell dinner. So many have gone on to create their own niche and starring roles within the restaurant world here and overseas, a testament to their talent and an achievement Margie and I are really proud of – the nurturing, guidance and shared experiences have paid off handsomely. I extend a big hand of thanks to all our staff who contributed to the success we enjoyed and accolades we received: for your commitment to our vision, for being valued team players and maintaining the rage.

Our customers and fans, where would we be without you! Thank you all for your support and loyalty, and for the many of you who visited me in London to experience East@West, and maybe even on to the next adventure when it arises. The mutual respect and understanding that develops and blossoms between restaurateur and customer is necessary for survival and for pushing the boundaries; it creates a relationship of trust and daring.

Providores of excellence help restaurateurs set the standard of excellence without compromise: you are all an essential part of my working life wherever I may be in the world. As I mentioned earlier, I have no tolerance for mediocrity, and this goes for the quality of every bit of produce I use in my cooking. Fabulous produce is the very best starting point when embarking on any cooking, so I recommend you heed that advice and apply it to your own culinary practice.

Finally, my ongoing gratitude goes to my publisher, Julie Gibbs, for her vision, persistence and style. We have travelled together over these many years, through several books, and I value and appreciate her guidance, tenacity and discipline. I firmly believe that the quality of anything produced is determined by the quality and integrity of those you collaborate with.

Pesto

Pesto is commonly known as the wonderfully pungent basil sauce that hailed originally from Genoa, Italy. When freshly made, its fragrance and taste is powerful and intoxicating, hence its popularity and widespread use in everyday cooking. The word 'pesto' refers to the method of preparation, where the ingredients are pounded together by hand in a mortar and pestle to make a paste. This time-consuming but rewarding process has been largely replaced by the mechanical food processor, making it a quick and simple task.

By adapting the literal meaning of the word, I use various forms of pesto in my cooking to give added depth and complexity to a particular dish. Basil Pine Nut Pesto, Coriander Peanut Pesto and Sun-dried Tomato Pesto are my staples and I always have them on hand at the Restaurant and at home for a ready-to-go snack or for more intricate use, as illustrated by the recipes that follow.

Pesto is at its best uncooked as its flavour changes when heated; it is tastiest when added at the last moment. The classic Basil Pine Nut Pesto can be served simply with ripe tomatoes, grilled meats or fish, pasta and hot potatoes or spooned over baked ricotta, added to roasted capsicum salad or spread onto bruschetta. The magic of basil pesto lies in its freshness and its direct association with the flavours of summer.

Coriander Peanut Pesto is made with Asian ingredients such as holy basil, coriander and mint spiked with a touch of chilli. Holy basil (also referred to as Thai or Asian basil) has a strong aniseed flavour and, used in this pesto preparation, its fresh and zesty flavour tantalises the tastebuds with the essence of the Orient. It is as versatile as its Mediterranean counterpart – simply spoon it over hot noodles or deep-fried seafood wontons or stir it into a light soup or broth. Try it out and expand your repertoire in the kitchen.

Sun-dried Tomato Pesto is another tasty addition to the larder. A recent phenomenon gives the popular use of sun-dried tomatoes with its origins in the Mediterranean. Its pungency gives a lift to an antipasto plate, pasta, grilled seafood or charcuterie items for a picnic.

Having these preparations on hand allows for a greater scope in producing something fabulous in a short amount of time. They are available for purchase at the Paramount Store ready to be eaten or used according to the whim of the buyer. However, should you feel inclined to start from scratch, these recipes are offered as a guide.

basil pine nut pesto

This is the universally well-known and original pesto that hails from Genoa in the Ligurian region of northern Italy. It keeps well for a month, refrigerated.

200 g basil leaves, washed
½ teaspoon sea salt
150 ml virgin olive oil
125 g pine nuts, lightly roasted
4 cloves garlic, minced
½ teaspoon black peppercorns, freshly ground
150 g parmesan cheese, freshly grated

1 In a food processor, blend the basil leaves with the salt and 50 ml of the olive oil until a paste has formed. Add the pine nuts, garlic and pepper and pulse to a paste.

2 Drizzle in the remaining olive oil with the motor running and process until smooth. Remove the paste from the processor bowl and gently stir in the parmesan cheese. Check the seasoning and adjust if necessary.

3 To store, spoon the pesto into a container, cover with a film of oil and seal. Keep refrigerated until ready to use.

coriander peanut pesto

This recipe uses the same method of preparation as that for the Basil Pine Nut Pesto but the Mediterranean flavours have been replaced by Asian ones; cheese, which is not part of the Asian repertoire, has been omitted. The pesto keeps well for a month, refrigerated.

200 ml peanut oil
40 g raw blanched peanuts
2 green bird's-eye chillies, minced
1 tablespoon freshly minced ginger
8 cloves garlic, minced
100 g holy basil leaves
25 g Vietnamese mint leaves
100 g coriander leaves
1 teaspoon shaved palm sugar
2 teaspoons fish sauce
20 ml fresh lime juice, strained

1 Heat the oil and roast the peanuts over medium heat until golden. Strain the peanuts from the oil and cool. Reserve both.

2 Blend the peanuts in a food processor with the chilli, ginger and garlic. Add the herbs and half the reserved oil and blend to form a smooth paste.

3 Add the sugar, fish sauce and lime juice and blend until the herbs are finely minced. Gradually pour in the remaining oil to make a smooth paste.

4 To store, spoon the pesto into a container, cover with a film of oil and seal. Keep refrigerated until ready to use.

sun-dried tomato pesto

For this recipe, I use sun-dried tomatoes that are packed in oil, so they need to be strained before being used. Alternatively, you can use tomatoes that you have oven-dried yourself. This is a very rich paste that has strong garlic overtones, so it is best used in moderation. The pesto keeps well for a month, refrigerated.

150 g ripe roma tomatoes, peeled and seeded
200 g sun-dried tomatoes
5 large cloves garlic
50 g sun-dried tomato paste
100 ml virgin olive oil
15 ml balsamic vinegar
15 ml red wine vinegar
½ teaspoon sea salt
½ teaspoon black peppercorns, freshly ground

1 Roughly chop the tomatoes, sun-dried tomatoes and garlic and blend with the sun-dried tomato paste in a food processor until smooth.

2 With the motor running, gradually add the olive oil in a thin stream. Add the vinegars and season to taste with the salt and pepper.

3 To store, spoon the pesto into a container, cover with a film of oil and seal. Keep refrigerated until ready to use.

chargrilled baby octopus with roasted capsicum, oven-dried tomatoes, olives and sun-dried tomato pesto

This dish celebrates the rich flavours of seafood, olive oil, garlic and tomatoes. The combination is a heady one and reminds us of the cuisines and cultures of other lands that have been brought to our doorstep. It is easy to execute as long as the basic preparations have been made beforehand and you have a good hot chargrill or barbecue at your disposal. The secret with the octopus lies in careful buying – be sure to look out for baby octopus, preferably from Port Lincoln, South Australia. Avoid the small, fully grown variety pummelled in cement mixers and often sold at fish markets as they do not become tender regardless of how carefully they have been cooked. Alternatively, braise a large octopus until just tender and toss it on the barbecue briefly before slicing it into bite-sized strips.

1 kg baby octopus, cleaned and head (and beak) removed
100 ml olive oil
a little freshly ground black pepper
6 tablespoons roasted red capsicum strips
3 tablespoons thinly sliced oven-dried tomatoes
2 tablespoons finely sliced red onion
18 kalamata olives, pitted and sliced lengthwise
2 tablespoons basil leaves, shredded
mizuna leaves, washed
6 teaspoons Sun-dried Tomato Pesto (see page 12)

Tomato Dressing
1 tablespoon sun-dried tomato paste
40 ml balsamic vinegar
120 ml virgin olive oil
½ teaspoon sea salt
½ teaspoon black peppercorns, freshly ground

1 Cut the octopus tentacles in half and marinate in the olive oil until ready to use. Season with black pepper.

2 To make the Tomato Dressing, whisk together the sun-dried tomato paste, balsamic vinegar, virgin olive oil, salt and pepper in a bowl until well incorporated.

3 In a large stainless steel bowl, mix together the roasted capsicum, oven-dried tomato, red onion, olives and basil. Pour on the dressing and mix well with a large spoon. Allow the bowl to warm gently at the edge of the chargrill or barbecue while the octopus is cooking.

4 Heat a chargrill or barbecue grill until very hot and then toss on the octopus. Distribute it evenly and cook quickly – the cooking will take only a couple of minutes. Use tongs to toss the octopus continuously to ensure even cooking without burning. The octopus will be cooked when the tentacles start to curl and the meat feels soft and tender to the touch – don't allow it to become firm or the meat will be overcooked.

5 Add the cooked octopus and mizuna leaves to the bowl, mix well and divide evenly between six plates. Spoon a teaspoon of Sun-dried Tomato Pesto on top of each and serve immediately. Alternatively, this dish can be served in one large bowl as part of a centre-table offering where guests can help themselves.

Serves 6

yamba prawn and saffron risotto with pesto

Risotto, one of my all-time favourites, is cooked regularly for our staff meals and at home as the ideal one-pot meal. It makes an appearance at the Restaurant as a special addition to the menu or as part of a set menu for a group. It is a dish that requires time, patience and constant attention to elevate it to its correct place. To cook and reheat it only results in a stodgy, sticky mess that dissatisfies the palate.

The basic rules for perfect risotto include using arborio rice, not a cheap substitute; frying the aromatic base and the rice first so that the rice is coated with fat, which allows the rice to swell and the hot liquid to be absorbed more readily; bringing the stock to simmering point and adding it gradually to the rice so that the cooking temperature remains even; careful and constant cooking, and serving the risotto as soon as it has been cooked. Making risotto is one of the most satisfying cooking and consuming processes in a culinary repertoire, so go ahead and experiment, keeping in mind the basic rules.

The Yamba prawns I recommend using here are caught along the coastline of northern New South Wales and sent directly to the Flying Squid Brothers in Sydney, avoiding the chemical and freezing treatment that usually occurs on the large prawn trawlers that may be at sea for up to a week or ten days. The freshness of these prawns shows in their taste and texture. When looking for prawns to cook, always choose green (uncooked) prawns that smell fresh and show no sign of blackening in the head.

900 ml fish stock
18 green Yamba king prawns
100 ml olive oil
2 tablespoons finely diced brown onion
2 teaspoons minced garlic
2 red bird's-eye chillies, minced
350 g arborio rice, rinsed
150 ml sauvignon blanc
1 teaspoon saffron threads
20 basil leaves, shredded
75 g unsalted butter
3 tablespoons Basil Pine Nut Pesto (see page 10)
1 teaspoon sea salt
1 teaspoon black peppercorns, freshly ground

1 Bring the fish stock to a boil in a saucepan and allow to maintain a gentle simmer.

2 Peel and clean the prawns then split each one in two.

3 Heat a wide-based braising pan and add the olive oil. Sauté the onion, garlic and chilli until the onion has softened and is golden. Add the rice and, stirring continuously, cook until it is coated with the oil.

4 Pour in the sauvignon blanc. As the wine is absorbed by the rice, add the saffron and start to ladle on the simmering fish stock, 150 ml at a time. Maintaining a fairly high heat, allow the rice to absorb the liquid before adding the next quantity and stir frequently to prevent the mixture from sticking. With each addition of stock, the rice will steam and swell to absorb the liquid. As you near the end of the stock the rice should still have a bit of bite in it; it will have become creamy but the grains will remain separate.

5 When the last ladle of stock has been absorbed, add the prawn meat and basil leaves, stirring constantly. Cook just until the prawns are translucent, then stir in the butter and pesto and season to taste with the salt and pepper.

6 Serve the risotto immediately with some chilled sauvignon blanc to accompany it.

Serves 6

deep-fried eggplant stuffed with coffin bay scallops, ginger and coriander with pesto dressing

This dish, a regular feature on the Paramount menu, is deceptively simple in appearance but a little time-consuming to make. It works beautifully as a dish because its texture, balance of flavours, method of cooking and its presentation make a great 'package'. For me, this dish epitomises the skill and craft of a professional cook in a technical and creative sense.

7 eggplants (8 cm in diameter)
18 large Coffin Bay scallops
1 egg white
1 teaspoon strained lemon juice
pinch of sea salt
pinch of freshly ground white pepper
20 ml single (35%) cream
2 egg yolks, beaten
1 tablespoon dried prawns, roasted and ground
vegetable oil for deep-frying

Smoked Eggplant Stuffing
3½ eggplants
vegetable oil
2 spring onions, finely sliced
2 coriander roots, finely sliced
2 teaspoons coriander leaves, chopped
1 teaspoon freshly minced ginger
½ teaspoon black peppercorns, freshly ground
1 teaspoon strained fresh lime juice
1 teaspoon fish sauce
½ teaspoon sesame oil

Pesto Dressing
50 ml fresh lime juice, strained
25 ml coconut vinegar
50 ml reduced tomato essence
25 ml fish sauce
1 teaspoon castor sugar
10 ml sesame oil
15 ml olive oil
3 tablespoons Basil Pine Nut Pesto (see page 10)

1 To make the Smoked Eggplant Stuffing, smoke and peel 3 of the eggplants. Squeeze out the excess juices and chop roughly.

2 Finely dice the remaining ½ eggplant. Deep-fry the diced eggplant until golden, then drain on paper towels. Combine the smoked and fried eggplant in a bowl. Add the remaining ingredients and mix well. Taste and adjust if necessary.

3 To prepare the 7 eggplants, cut 12 thin rounds from one of the eggplants. Brush with a little vegetable oil and chargrill on each side.

4 Cut the tops and bottoms off the remaining 6 eggplants to leave a trunk on each one that is 8 cm high. Cut a 3 mm slice off the top end of each eggplant and reserve for later use as lids.

5 Take an eggplant and sit it upright. Use a 5 cm round pastry cutter to press down through the centre of the eggplant trunk until 1 cm from the bottom. Using a small paring knife, make a 2 cm long horizontal incision into the side of the eggplant 1 cm up from the base. Move the knife from side to side to loosen the 'core'. Be careful not to pierce the other side of the eggplant. Remove the core to form a well in the centre of the eggplant trunk. Repeat with the remaining eggplants.

6 Blend 6 of the scallops in the chilled bowl of a food processor with the egg white, lemon juice, salt and white pepper until smooth. Add the cream and pulse until just incorporated. Do not overwork this paste or it will separate – it must hold together to act as a 'glue'. Slice each of the remaining scallops into 3 discs, leaving the coral intact.

7 To make the Pesto Dressing, mix together all the ingredients except the pesto and stir well. Taste and adjust, if necessary, and set aside.

8 To assemble, rub a small amount of the scallop paste around the inside of the eggplant's cavity, especially over the small incision that was made with the paring knife. Position a slice of grilled eggplant on the bottom of the cavity and spoon in Smoked Eggplant Stuffing until a little over half full. Cover the stuffing with 6 fanned-out scallop discs. Top the scallops with another grilled eggplant slice and seal with the scallop paste. Brush with the beaten egg yolk and press on the reserved lid. Brush the top of the lid with egg yolk and sprinkle on a little of the ground prawns.

9 Repeat this process with the other 5 eggplant trunks. Allow the stuffed eggplants to set in the refrigerator for 3 hours before cooking.

10 To cook the prepared eggplants, heat a deep-fryer or 5 litre stockpot with enough vegetable oil to cover the eggplants. When the oil reaches 180°C, cook the eggplants for 8 minutes, ensuring they remain submerged in the oil. I use wooden skewers threaded across the deep-fryer's wire basket to keep them in place. (It may be necessary to cook the eggplants 2 or 3 at a time, depending on the size of the pot.) Carefully remove the eggplants from the oil with a flat slide or spatula and drain on paper towels momentarily before plating.

11 Mix together the dressing and pesto, and spoon over and around each eggplant. Serve immediately.

Serves 6

eggplant, goat's cheese and pesto sandwich

This dish was born in the early days of the Paragon kitchen, when we were new kids on the block, and still makes regular appearances on the Paramount menu. Its success lies in the combination of flavours and its last-minute cooking and assembly. Its construction is a play on the concept of a sandwich, where the eggplant takes on the role of bread and simply transforms a classic idea into a more theatrical presentation. The underlying intention is that when you cut through the sandwich from top to bottom your mouth is assaulted with all the flavours and textures at once. Another endearing feature of this dish is that it's as easy to put together as a regular sandwich and the mini version, using Japanese eggplants, makes an interesting appetiser or canapé.

3 eggplants
sea salt
vegetable oil for deep-frying
30 ml balsamic vinegar
90 ml virgin olive oil
extra pinch of sea salt
pinch of freshly ground black pepper
300 g Kervella or Milawa fresh goat's cheese, at room temperature
2 roasted red capsicums, cut into strips lengthwise
9 teaspoons Basil Pine Nut Pesto (see page 10)
3 tablespoons finely shredded rocket leaves

1 Cut the eggplants into 12 × 2 cm thick slices, sprinkle with salt and leave to sweat on a dry tray for 1 hour. Dry with paper towels to remove any excess moisture and salt.

2 Heat the vegetable oil in a deep-fryer or large saucepan to 180°C and fry the eggplant slices until golden brown on both sides. Drain, then pat dry with paper towels.

3 Make a vinaigrette by whisking together the balsamic vinegar, virgin olive oil and the extra salt and the pepper.

4 To assemble the sandwiches, cut the goat's cheese into 6 × 1 cm thick slices. Put a slice of eggplant on a plate and top with a slice of goat's cheese. Cover the cheese with a few strips of the roasted capsicum and then add 1 teaspoon of the pesto. Drizzle over some vinaigrette and then sprinkle on some of the finely shredded rocket leaves. Cover with another slice of eggplant and top this with a little extra pesto, vinaigrette and shredded rocket. Repeat this process using the remaining ingredients to make 6 sandwiches.

5 Serve immediately, while the eggplant is hot.

Serves 6

Eggplant, Goat's Cheese and Pesto Sandwich

stir-fried pacific oysters and seaweed noodles with bok choy and coriander peanut pesto

Here's a fabulous way to present oysters that have been literally just warmed through by a fast application of heat. The combined flavours have a strong association with the iodine headiness of the sea. Its size, fresh, salty sea flavour and ability to take a quick show of heat without shrinking away to nothing make the large Pacific oyster ideal for this preparation. The only trick with this dish is to cook each serve separately as the small quantities ensure that ingredients heat through quickly without lowering the temperature of the wok and the oysters do not overcook. You will need 12 bowls to prepare this dish; the secret to cooking this dish successfully lies in quick cooking. Cook two or three serves at a time and rest the cooked serves briefly while cooking the next batch. Small Teflon woks, which make cooking this dish a breeze, are available from Asian food stores.

36 large Pacific oysters, unshucked
12 bok choy hearts
2 large green chillies
3 teaspoons Pickled Ginger, finely sliced (see page 52)
3 tablespoons coriander leaves
6 spring onions, cut into 1 cm rounds
125 g snow pea sprouts
6 teaspoons Coriander Peanut Pesto (see page 11)

Seaweed Noodles
250 g bread flour
½ teaspoon sea salt
2 nori seaweed sheets, toasted, chopped and ground
3 large (61 g) eggs
2 teaspoons virgin olive oil
rice flour

Oyster Dressing
200 ml reserved oyster juices
160 ml fish stock
20 ml fish sauce
10 ml light soy sauce
20 ml mirin
60 ml tamarind juice
30 ml fresh lime juice, strained

1 To make the Seaweed Noodles, mix together the flour, salt and ground seaweed in a food processor. With the motor running, add the eggs and the oil and process until the dough comes together to form a ball. Wrap the dough in plastic foodwrap and refrigerate for 1 hour.

2 Cut the chilled dough into 4 portions to make it easier to handle and roll out each piece on a cool, flat surface sprinkled with fine rice flour. (The rice flour makes the dough pass through the rollers on the pasta machine easily without tearing. The gluten-free rice flour is used so that no extra gluten, which would toughen the dough, is introduced.) Pass each piece of dough through the rollers on a pasta machine, starting at the thickest setting and working through to the thinnest setting. Dust the sheets of dough each time with rice flour so they do not become sticky and unmanageable. Pass the thin sheets of pasta through the spaghetti cutters on the machine.

3 Bring a large saucepan of water to a rolling boil. Cook the noodles for 2 minutes. Remove the noodles from the boiling water and refresh under cold, running water. Drain and dress with a little olive oil to prevent them from sticking together.

4 Shuck the oysters and reserve all the strained juices for the dressing. Refrigerate the oysters and their juices until ready to use.

5 To make the Oyster Dressing, mix together all the ingredients in a bowl (if necessary, top up the oyster juices with fish stock to make 200 ml). Taste and adjust if necessary. Keep refrigerated until ready to use.

6 Trim the bok choy hearts of any limp or broken outer leaves, leaving the stem and leaves intact so they do not separate during cooking. Rinse under cold water. Steam the bok choy hearts for 3 minutes in the tray of a metal Chinese steamer or a bamboo basket until softened. Refresh immediately in a bowl of iced water.

7 Remove the seeds and membrane from the chillies and cut the flesh into fine julienne.

8 To assemble, divide the noodles, bok choy and dressing between six bowls and the remaining ingredients between another six bowls.

9 Heat the woks over a high heat and add the first preparation of noodles, dressing and bok choy to each. Toss over the heat until warmed, being careful that the noodles don't stick. Add a bowl of the second preparation, which includes the oysters, to each wok, stir with tongs to combine quickly and toss over the heat until warmed through, about 1 minute. Pile the noodles onto serving plates and repeat the cooking process. Serve immediately.

Serves 6

crispy duck and scallop rice-paper rolls with coriander peanut pesto

This recipe takes its lead from the Vietnamese-style spring roll, cha giò, *and gives it a refreshing lift with the addition of the Coriander Peanut Pesto. You can prepare the duck according to the recipe for Five-spice Duck and Shiitake Mushroom Pies with Ginger Glaze (see page 98) or simply buy a roast duck from an Asian food store.*

50 g cellophane noodles
9 tablespoons Coriander Peanut Pesto (see page 11)
3 large eggs
25 ml fish sauce
½ teaspoon finely ground black pepper
125 g cooked duck meat, finely chopped
125 g scallop meat, minced
50 g water chestnuts
1 small carrot, peeled and finely shredded
3 spring onions, sliced into fine rounds
½ small cucumber, peeled, seeded and finely shredded
2 teaspoons Vietnamese mint leaves, shredded
2 teaspoons coriander leaves
24 round rice-paper wrappers
egg wash
oil for deep-frying

1 Blanch the cellophane noodles in boiling water for 1 minute. Refresh under cold water and strain. Slice the noodles into 2 cm lengths and mix in a bowl with 3 tablespoons of the Coriander Peanut Pesto.

2 Whisk the eggs, fish sauce and pepper together. Add to the noodles with all the other ingredients except the rice-paper wrappers. Mix thoroughly.

3 Soak a rice-paper wrapper in a large bowl of warm water until it softens and becomes pliable. Lay the softened wrappers on a clean cloth. Fold over the bottom edge of the wrapper towards the centre and place 2 tablespoons of filling on the folded portion. Roll over once, fold in the edges and roll over again. Brush the edges with egg wash to secure. Rest the roll on its seam on a tray lined with absorbent paper until ready to cook. Repeat until all the wrappers are used.

4 Heat the oil in a deep-fryer or a deep saucepan until it reaches 160°C. Fry the rolls, 6 at a time (to avoid lowering the temperature), for 8 minutes until pale golden. Remove from the oil and drain on paper towels. Keep the rolls warm in the oven while you cook the remaining rolls. Don't have the frying oil too hot or the rolls will burn and split; rice paper is more fragile than regular spring roll pastry.

5 Serve the rice-paper rolls with the remaining Coriander Peanut Pesto.

Serves 6

Preserved Lemons

The versatile lemon plays an integral role in the culinary process – the skin, seeds, juice and flesh all contribute in their own right and collectively to the chemistry of food. The lemon activates change – it is the revolutionary of the food world. The lemon has a major role as a flavour enhancer and it doesn't come out of a bottle! As a fresh ingredient, the lemon has great longevity or shelf life but, of course, it is best when freshly picked and ripe. Many cuisines of the world use the lemon to balance richness, to preserve food or to add a necessary zest or lift to a dish. In addition, the lemon is a wonderful source of vitamin C, a most necessary part of our diet.

Maximise resources during times of abundance and preserve lemons when they are at their best, and enjoy their special characters through to the next season. Often used in conjunction with aromatic spices and herbs, preserved lemons provide an antidote to the richness of meat and the oiliness of fish and olives, at the same time as transforming an acceptable dish into a taste sensation.

Historically linked with the cuisine of Morocco, preserved lemons are part of the staple diet of that country and give a unique perfume and pickled taste to the foods with which they are cooked. Their yellowness and firm shape is retained as they rest glistening in their salty preserving liquid, dispelling their potent acidity and changing the taste we most usually associate with this member of the citrus family to a more mellow, musky and syrupy flavour.

We preserve lemons at the Restaurant twice a year – during autumn and spring when the fruit is plentiful, juicy and cheap. We stock Preserved Lemons at our Store so that last-minute decisions can be made by the home cook who can use them in a variety of ways: to spike a lamb stew, as part of a garlic and onion stuffing for a barbecued fish, to flavour a rice pilaf, to add to a sizzling plate of garlic prawns or mushrooms or to give a lift to a seafood salad.

Spices symbolise luxury and, as good cooking is luxurious, I adopt the principle that spices should be used generously and wholeheartedly. This philosophy is particularly evident in the recipes of this chapter as the combination of preserved lemons with rich and varied spices seems a natural one. Don't look to these recipes when trying to whip together a last-minute dinner without preserved lemons to hand, however, as there is no substitute. Lemon juice or zest will not suffice.

preserved lemons

Important tips to remember when preserving lemons include choosing ripe, fragrant fruit, ensuring the lemons are washed thoroughly before salting, covering the lemons completely with liquid during storage and keeping them refrigerated once opened. Once preserved, the lemons need to be stored for 6 weeks before use and keep for 12 months.

10 ripe thin-skinned lemons
150 g fine table salt
1 litre lemon juice (about 20 lemons)

1 Wash the lemons thoroughly, scrubbing the skins if necessary. Cut the lemons into quarters lengthwise to within 1 cm of the base. Pack each lemon with salt and reshape the fruit by pressing the quarters back together.

2 Place the lemons into a 2 litre preserving jar and sprinkle with a little extra salt. Pour in the lemon juice until the lemons are covered. Seal the jar and store the lemons for 6 weeks in a cool place away from direct light.

3 When the lemons are ready to use, remove from the jar as needed and rinse with water. Discard the flesh and use the preserved lemon as required. Refrigerate the opened jar.

hot pot of slow-braised beef brisket with preserved lemons and waxy potatoes

This is a perfect heart-warming, cold-weather dish that requires a time-honoured, slow-cooking process to extract maximum flavour from all the ingredients. We serve it during the winter months presented in a clay pot with couscous dressed with Preserved Lemon Gremolata on the plate so that the diner can make a real feast of it. The richness is ambrosial.

2 kg beef brisket
200 ml olive oil
2 brown onions, finely diced
6 cloves garlic, minced
1 tablespoon freshly minced ginger
1 red bird's-eye chilli, minced
2 teaspoons ras el hanout (see page 162)
1 teaspoon cummin seeds, roasted and ground
2 teaspoons coriander seeds, roasted and ground
2 dried large red chillies, roasted and ground
1 teaspoon hot paprika
2 teaspoons black peppercorns, freshly ground
3 litres light beef or veal stock
1 Preserved Lemon, finely chopped (see page 24)
1 teaspoon sea salt
9 waxy potatoes (patronne or pink fir apple), parboiled
750 ml chicken stock
50 g unsalted butter
500 g couscous grains
extra sea salt
extra freshly ground black pepper

Preserved Lemon Gremolata
½ cup flat parsley leaves, chopped
1 tablespoon finely diced red onion
2 cloves garlic, minced
2 teaspoons finely diced Preserved Lemon (see page 24)

1 Put a roasting pan in the oven and preheat to 140°C. Brush the beef brisket with some of the olive oil and sprinkle with a little black pepper. Seal the meat in the hot roasting pan in the oven (this will take about 10 minutes on each side to allow it to brown).

2 Remove the meat (but leave the oven on) and, in the same pan, add the rest of the olive oil. Sauté the onion, garlic, ginger and chilli on the stove top until fragrant. Add the spices and cook for a few minutes. Pour in the beef stock and bring it to a boil. Reduce to a simmer, add the browned beef brisket and cover with foil.

3 Return the meat to the oven for 3 hours, or until the meat is very tender. Turn the meat in the stock during the cooking process. After 2 hours of cooking, stir half the Preserved Lemon into the stock. When the meat is ready, remove the pan from the oven and take the meat out of the stock. Rest the meat until it is cool enough to handle.

4 Pass the stock through a fine-mesh sieve, saving the onion and lemon mixture to add later to the reduced stock. Bring the strained stock to a boil in a saucepan and allow to reduce by half until the sauce thickens and becomes unctuous but not sticky. Add the reserved onion and lemon mixture, the remaining lemon and the salt to the sauce. Taste for seasoning and adjust if necessary. (The lemon usually provides enough salt to balance and enhance the meat but a little extra pepper may be required.)

5 Carefully prepare the brisket by removing any fat, bones, tendons and muscle tissue and cut the meat into large chunks so it doesn't fall apart when it is reheated in the sauce. Bring the finished sauce to a boil with the parboiled potatoes, reduce the heat and add the meat. Simmer very gently for 10 minutes.

6 Prepare the couscous by bringing the chicken stock to a boil and adding it with the butter to the couscous grains in a large bowl. Season with salt and pepper and stir. Allow the grains to absorb the liquid. Put the bowl in a steamer and steam for 5 minutes.

7 Just before serving, finely mince the Gremolata ingredients together with a cleaver.

8 To serve, spoon some couscous onto each plate and add the meat, potatoes and sauce and sprinkle with gremolata. Alternatively, the couscous can be placed in a large bowl in the middle of the table with the meat in another bowl and everyone can help themselves to give the meal a more informal tone.

Serves 6

rare roasted squab with saffron, green olives and preserved lemon

Squabs are delectable birds and their meat holds up very well to rich, spicy flavours. Squab meat is at its best when cooked rare, when it is at its juiciest and tastiest. I am quite adamant that particular meats should never be overcooked. I would rather people choose something else if they are turned off by the relaxed nature of rare meat than have them disappointed by the texture of overcooked meat and laying that responsibility with the cook. The generic steak house can play that role but we, as restaurateurs, have a greater responsibility in the education and understanding of the palate.
The squabs can be served with either couscous or a crisp potato galette. Individual finger bowls provide a finishing touch.

2 teaspoons hot paprika
2 teaspoons turmeric powder, roasted
2 teaspoons cummin seeds, roasted and ground
120 ml olive oil
6 × 400 g squabs
30 g ghee
24 red shallots, peeled
6 cloves garlic, minced
2 teaspoons freshly minced ginger
100 g squab livers
1.5 litres squab or game stock
12 large green olives, pitted and quartered
1 teaspoon saffron threads
1 Preserved Lemon, finely chopped (see page 24)
30 ml lemon juice, strained
½ teaspoon black pepper, freshly ground
40 g unsalted butter
1 tablespoon coriander leaves

1 Mix half the paprika, turmeric and cummin with the olive oil. Clean and prepare the squabs and brush inside and out with the spiced olive oil.

2 Slice 12 of the shallots. In a large saucepan, fry the sliced shallots, garlic, ginger and squab livers in the ghee over moderate heat until softened and aromatic. Add the remaining paprika, turmeric and cummin and cook for 2 minutes.

3 Add the stock to the saucepan and bring to a boil. Reduce the heat and simmer gently until the stock has reduced by half and has developed a rich colour and taste. Skim regularly with a mesh spoon. Pass the sauce through a fine-mesh sieve, pressing firmly to extract all juices.

4 Bring the strained sauce to a boil, add the remaining whole shallots and simmer for 15 minutes until the shallots have softened. Add the olives, saffron and lemon and simmer for a further 5 minutes. (The sauce can be made to this stage ahead of time and finished off as you are ready to serve when the squabs have been roasted.)

5 Preheat the oven to 300°C or as high as your oven will go. To cook the squabs, place the birds, breast-side down, in a cast-iron frying pan or dish and roast for 8 minutes. Remove from the oven and allow to rest in a warm place for 10 minutes to allow the juices to settle.

6 To serve, carve the breasts off the bone and slice each breast in half diagonally. Remove the legs from each carcass and leave whole (reserve the carcasses to make extra stock later). Finish the sauce by whisking in the lemon juice, pepper and butter, to give it a gloss, and stir in the coriander leaves.

7 Place 2 legs in the centre of each serving plate and arrange the 4 pieces of breast meat on top. Pour the sauce around the meat and serve immediately.

Serves 6

Rare Roasted Squab with Saffron, Green Olives and Preserved Lemon

baked quails stuffed with rice, pine nuts and preserved lemons with a spiced tomato sauce

This recipe is another popular adaptation of the flavours of northern Africa suited to our style of cooking. The most difficult part of this preparation is boning out the quails but if you can buy them already boned, the rest is relatively easy. This dish is quite versatile in that it can be served as an entrée (1 bird each) or as a main course (2 birds each) or as part of a centre-table spread where there are many things to taste.

100 ml olive oil
3 tablespoons finely minced brown onion
1 tablespoon minced garlic
seeds of 4 cardamom pods, ground
1 teaspoon ground cinnamon
1½ cups cooked long grain rice
150 g pine nuts, lightly roasted
3 tablespoons flat parsley leaves, shredded
1 Preserved Lemon, finely chopped (see page 24)
1 teaspoon sea salt
2 teaspoons black peppercorns, freshly ground
24 prepared vine leaves
12 large quails, boned out
2 litres chicken stock

Spicy Tomato Sauce
8 large, ripe tomatoes
5 cloves garlic, unpeeled
250 ml olive oil
1 brown onion, minced
1 stick cinnamon
2 teaspoons cummin seeds, roasted and ground
1 teaspoon black peppercorns, cracked
200 ml white wine

1 To make the Spicy Tomato Sauce, preheat the oven to 250°C. Roast the tomatoes and garlic in a baking pan for about 30 minutes or until the tomatoes are coloured and split open.

2 Heat a wide-based braising pan and add 100 ml of the olive oil and fry the onion until softened and aromatic, stirring to prevent it sticking and burning. Add the cinnamon stick, ground cummin and cracked black peppercorns and stir until fragrant. Add the roasted tomatoes, garlic and the white wine and simmer gently for 30 minutes.

3 Remove the pan from the heat and pass the sauce through a fine conical sieve. Pour the sauce into the bowl of a food processor. With the motor running, slowly pour in the remaining olive oil in a thin stream to emulsify the sauce. Check the seasoning and adjust with sea salt and pepper if necessary. Set the sauce aside until required.

4 To prepare the stuffing for the quails, heat the olive oil in a frying pan and gently sauté the onion and garlic without colouring. Add the cardamom and cinnamon to the pan, stirring to mix. Remove from the heat. Stir in the cooked rice, pine nuts, parsley, lemon, salt and pepper and allow to cool.

5 Wash the vine leaves to remove the brine. Stuff the quails with the cooled rice mixture and wrap each quail around its middle with 2 vine leaves, securing them with a skewer.

6 Sit the quails in a single layer in a wide-based braising pan that is just large enough to hold the birds snugly. Bring the chicken stock to a boil in another saucepan and pour over the quails to cover. Cover with a lid and simmer gently for 10 minutes until the quails are pink. The quails are done if the juices run clear with a touch of pink when a skewer is inserted into the breast.

7 Preheat the oven to 250°C.

8 Take the braising pan off the heat and remove the quails gently from the stock with a slotted spoon. Sit the quails on a baking tray and crisp in the hot oven for 4 minutes. Reheat the sauce, if necessary, while the birds are baking.

9 Remove the skewers, place the quails on serving plates and spoon the hot sauce over and around the birds.

Serves 6 or 12

tasmanian salmon fillet baked in chermoula with preserved lemon and buttered spinach

This dish was on our first Paramount menu and continues to make regular appearances, particularly in the warmer summer months when the Tasmanian salmon is at its best. The flavours are not cloying or rich – the emphasis is on the freshness of all the components – and the chermoula marinade provides an aromatic presence that blends perfectly with the luscious spinach. The whole thing has a melt-in-the mouth sensation. The flesh and flavour of the freshwater salmon from Victoria's Yarra Valley that has recently come onto the market is equal in the quality to that of its ocean cousin and works just as well in this recipe. Make sure that the fillets are taken from the thickest part of the fish. The chermoula can be made up to 3 days in advance.

6 × 200 g salmon fillets
3 bunches of spinach leaves, stalks removed
75 g unsalted butter
½ teaspoon sea salt
½ teaspoon black peppercorns, freshly ground
pinch of freshly grated nutmeg
½ Preserved Lemon, finely chopped (see page 24)
60 ml virgin olive oil

Preserved Lemon Chermoula
4 large cloves garlic
2 red bird's-eye chillies
10 red shallots, finely sliced lengthwise
¼ cup flat parsley leaves, finely chopped
½ cup coriander leaves, finely chopped
½ cup spearmint leaves, finely chopped
1 teaspoon cummin seeds, roasted and ground
½ teaspoon black peppercorns, freshly ground
1 Preserved Lemon, finely chopped (see page 24)
200 ml virgin olive oil

1 To make the chermoula, mince the garlic and chillies together. Mix the shallots, herbs, spices and lemon in a bowl and stir in the olive oil to bind the mixture together. Refrigerate until ready to use.

2 To prepare the fish, cut 6 sheets of baking paper and 6 sheets of foil, each 20 cm square. Remove any bones in the salmon fillets with a pair of tweezers. Spread 1 tablespoon of chermoula onto each piece of baking paper, and position a piece of salmon on it. Spread another tablespoon of chermoula on top of the fish. Fold each piece of paper over to make a secure package and then wrap in a foil square. Allow the salmon parcels to marinate in the refrigerator for 3–5 hours before cooking.

3 Wash the spinach leaves thoroughly and blanch in boiling water for 30 seconds. Refresh immediately in iced water to stop the cooking process and retain the colour. Squeeze out all excess water and set aside.

4 Preheat the oven to 200°C and bake the salmon fillets in their foil parcels on a baking tray for 6–8 minutes, depending on their thickness. The fish should retain a rosy blush in the middle and not be cooked right through as it has a tendency to dry out. (Fish, like meat, is best served rare to get full benefit of flavour and texture.)

5 While the fish is baking, heat a frying pan and melt the butter gently. Add the spinach, salt, pepper and nutmeg and stir continuously over a medium heat until the spinach softens and warms through. Don't let it burn or become crisp.

6 Stir the chopped Preserved Lemon into the virgin olive oil.

7 When the fish is ready, remove it from the oven and unwrap the parcels. Spoon the spinach onto serving plates and slide the fish on top. Pour over the excess juices from the parcels. Spoon over the lemon and oil and serve immediately.

Serves 6

Chilli Pastes

I can't imagine cooking without the beloved chilli, life would be too boring and dull. Chillies are a flamboyant element of the cooking process. They create heat, fire and really get the palate going. As a raw ingredient, they are a symbol of strength and versatility. The origin of the chilli can be traced back to South America well before trade routes were established. Today the use of chillies in cooking can be found in many cuisines of the world. They have become an essential and indispensable ingredient in the historical development of food. There are many varieties of chilli, each giving a specific flavour, pungency, aroma and heat. For the regular chilli consumer, their taste is addictive.

When selecting chillies, the basic guideline is that size determines heat: the smaller they are, the hotter they are, with most of the heat being stored in the seeds and membrane. Green chillies are usually hotter as they sweeten slightly as they ripen to a red colour. Chillies that grow in a hot tropical climate tend to give off the most heat. Tolerance to their heat grows with use, so the best advice to give when reading or cooking a particular recipe is to taste the chilli carefully in its raw state first to determine how much to use. Chillies deserve to be used in a proper context, not thrown in haphazardly without any basic understanding of their effect on the finished product – that is tantamount to abuse and indiscriminate use displays ignorance for the fundamental aspects of cooking. Their diversity lies in their many varieties and possible cooking treatments. They can be used raw, fried, stewed, smoked, dried, roasted, ground, grilled or stuffed. They also form the bases for oils, pastes, sambals, sauces, preserves and spice mixes.

The use of chilli in current cooking methods in Australia has a direct relationship with the development of our food culture. Our white history is one of immigrant status, where each ethnic group has brought with it its particular cooking style and ingredients. These practices have been adopted and adapted to suit our changing needs and desires. The emergence of an identifiable Australian food culture and cuisine develops as we grow confident enough not to rely on borrowed terms to define what we are doing in terms of professional technique and everyday cooking and eating. Chillies have become part of our diet: they grow abundantly, suit our climate, are good for our health, are no longer deemed foreign, are readily obtainable and feature on restaurant, bistro and café menus across the country. As a group of people, Australians have become much more adventurous eaters. Chillies can even spark philosophical, political and social debate – such is their strength!

At the Paramount, chillies show their faces in many preparations, sometimes with subtlety, sometimes with strength. As cooks, we embrace them with passion. We keep on hand four types of fresh chilli at any one time, not allowing for the imported American/Mexican dried varieties that are also used in abundance. Their dried state reduces some of their heat but heightens other facets of their flavours. We use mostly the green or red bird's-eye chillies, the small Asian variety commonly found in the shops, and the longer and larger, not-so-hot, red or green chillies. When available, we also sparingly use a tiny chilli that has enormous heat. According to my learned colleague David Thompson of Sydney's Darley Street Thai Restaurant, its Thai name *prik kii noo suan* means 'garden mouse chilli', but it is commonly referred to as the 'scud' chilli by aficionados. Apparently, in Queensland, where they are grown, they are referred to as 'ornamental chillies'.

When using any type of chilli, it is important to remember it must balance with the other flavours and not override them, so don't let the heat kill the palate. Chilli should be detectable for its fragrance as well as its heat. Experimentation is the key to understanding and gaining confidence with chilli – make it work for you and you will have a friend forever.

We make a variety of chilli pastes for use in dishes offered in the Restaurant and some of these are duplicated for purchase in the Store.

chilli jam

Chilli jam is always on hand at home and in the Restaurant because of its versatility and is a favourite with some as a simple spread on toast (mind you, a healthy chilli appetite and tolerance is needed to cope with this method of consumption). It can be simmered in coconut cream and used as a sauce for fish or chicken; it can be spooned over grilled meat, or used as part of a marinade. Use it as you would any other chilli sambal. Chilli jam keeps for 3 months, refrigerated.

1.5 kg large red chillies
300 g red bird's-eye chillies
8 large brown onions
15 large cloves garlic
1 litre vegetable oil
300 ml tamarind juice
125 g palm sugar, shaved

1 Chop the chillies, onions and garlic and then blend in a food processor to a fine paste with the oil.

2 Cook the chilli mixture in a heavy, wide-based braising pan on a low heat until the paste changes colour to a dark red. This will take up to 12 hours of continuous slow cooking.

3 Add the tamarind juice and the palm sugar to the chilli paste and cook for a further 2 hours on very low heat.

4 To store, spoon the jam into jars, cover with oil, seal and refrigerate.

lemongrass and chilli paste

This most fragrant paste brings a simple stir-fry to life and gives food a fiery zing. The flavours are released immediately with the application of heat and respond better to a quick, high blast than a slower approach, which only results in a stewy mess. This paste wins the popularity stakes at the Store as the biggest-selling item. Customers feel comfortable using it and stir-frying has become one of the most common cooking methods in the domestic arena these days. This paste keeps for 2 months, refrigerated.

10 stalks lemongrass
12 red bird's-eye chillies
15 cloves garlic
8 coriander roots
6 fresh kaffir lime leaves
200 ml vegetable oil
3 teaspoons black peppercorns, freshly ground
50 ml fish sauce

1 Finely chop the lemongrass, chillies, garlic, coriander roots and lime leaves (doing this before blending the ingredients makes a finer paste).

2 Blend the chopped ingredients in a food processor with the oil. Add the pepper and fish sauce and blend until the paste is quite fine. Check for taste and adjust if necessary.

3 To store, spoon into a jar, cover with oil, seal and refrigerate.

harissa

Like chilli jam, harissa can be eaten as is. It is the North African counterpart of the Asian sambals, though very much hotter as it has not been mellowed with cooking or by the addition of sugar. Harissa is a relish served as an enhancer of salads, cooked fish and meats and is an automatic addition to couscous. Test the water, so to speak, and then use accordingly. Harissa seems to keep, refrigerated, forever!

75 g dried large red chillies, chopped
100 ml water
2 large cloves garlic, minced
2 teaspoons cummin seeds, roasted and ground
1/4 teaspoon caraway seeds, ground
1 teaspoon sea salt
50 ml tomato purée
60 ml olive oil

1 Soak the chopped chilli in the water for 2 hours.

2 Blend the chilli, water and garlic in a food processor to a purée. Add the spices, salt and tomato purée and blend well. With the motor running, slowly pour in the olive oil and mix thoroughly.

3 To store, spoon into a jar, cover with oil, seal and refrigerate.

laksa paste

This chilli paste has its origins in the Nyonya cooking of Malaysia and Singapore, food that is renowned for it heady spiciness and richness. Laksa paste needs to be cooked to make it palatable and desirable. The heat brings out the subtlety of the flavours as they infuse the added liquid, usually stock and coconut milk. It is a great paste to have on hand to throw together a fabulous soup at the last minute and it keeps for 1 month, refrigerated.

2 teaspoons belacan (shrimp paste)
2 small red onions, chopped
4 cloves garlic, sliced
1 teaspoon lime zest
1 stalk lemongrass, finely sliced
1 teaspoon freshly chopped galangal
1 teaspoon freshly chopped turmeric
4 red bird's-eye chillies
25 g candlenuts
1 teaspoon dried prawns, roasted and ground
2 dried chillies, roasted and ground
1 teaspoon coriander seeds, roasted and ground
2 coriander roots, chopped
1 teaspoon turmeric powder
1 tablespoon coriander leaves
1 tablespoon Vietnamese mint leaves
120 ml vegetable oil

1 Dry-roast the belacan in a frying pan over a medium heat. (This brings out the flavour of the paste.) Blend all the ingredients together in a food processor until a smooth paste forms.

2 To store, spoon into a jar, cover with oil, seal and refrigerate.

aromatic curry paste

Curry has become a common element of everyday cooking in Australia. Long gone are the Anglo-Saxon bastardisations, where everything from canned pineapple, apple, sultanas and cream were added to the bland curry powders that were synonymous with the 'exotic' cooking of the fifties and sixties. Our shelves have been invaded with myriad choices and we are learning about the subtleties of curry flavours as well as developing an understanding of their complexities and origins.

The making of curry powders and pastes is considered an art in Asian countries: the blending of spices is the essence of cooking in India, just as curry pastes are of prime importance in Thai cooking.

Combinations vary according to regions and the types of food they are to be cooked with and all are distinctive. This particular curry paste is inspired by the flavours of southern India and the combination of spices makes for a heady, aromatic and slightly sweet concoction. It can simply be infused in coconut milk, along with your desired choice of protein, or used as a marinade for meat or fish to be barbecued or grilled. This curry paste keeps for 2 months, refrigerated.

1 large brown onion, finely diced
3 cloves garlic, minced
1 tablespoon freshly minced young ginger
40 ml vegetable oil
2 teaspoons turmeric powder
2 teaspoons dried red chillies, roasted and ground
2 teaspoons cummin seeds, roasted and ground
3 teaspoons coriander seeds, roasted and ground
1 teaspoon white peppercorns
pinch of freshly grated nutmeg
seeds of 2 cardamom pods, ground
100 ml tomato purée
4 ripe tomatoes, peeled and roughly diced
200 ml coconut cream
1 stick cinnamon
10 fresh curry leaves
50 ml fish sauce

1 Fry the onion, garlic and ginger in the oil in a wide-based frying pan until softened and aromatic. Add the spices and stir over the heat until they become fragrant. Stir in the tomato purée and diced tomato and cook until soft.

2 Pour in the coconut cream and add the cinnamon and curry leaves. Cook, uncovered, for 20 minutes on a low to medium heat, stirring often to prevent sticking, until the paste thickens. Add the fish sauce, taste and adjust if necessary.

3 To store, spoon into jars and refrigerate.

spiced tomato and chilli pickle

This paste is of Indian origin and rich in spices and the sweetness of the tomatoes is balanced by the gentle heat of the chilli. It is an adaptation of the tomato kasaundi in Charmaine Solomon's Complete Asian Cookbook. *It is a variation of the traditional tomato chutney, pickle or relish served as a condiment with Indian breads and fish dishes. The paste has the appearance of chutney and has the sweet-sour-spicy characteristic of Indian preserves. It is made even more luscious when a lashing of butter is quickly stirred into it once it has been heated. This pickle keeps well for 2 months, refrigerated.*

1 tablespoon brown mustard seeds
125 ml cider vinegar
2 teaspoons turmeric powder
pinch of ground cloves
2 tablespoons cummin seeds, roasted and ground
125 ml vegetable oil
2 tablespoons freshly minced ginger
10 cloves garlic
10 red bird's-eye chillies
2 kg ripe tomatoes, peeled and quartered
75 g palm sugar, shaved
60 ml fish sauce

1 In a small saucepan, cook the mustard seeds in the vinegar for 10 minutes. Remove from the heat and allow to cool for 2 hours.

2 In a large saucepan, fry the turmeric, cloves and cummin gently in the oil until fragrant.

3 Purée the ginger, garlic, chillies, mustard seeds and vinegar in a food processor until smooth and add to the oil and spices with the tomato quarters. Cook for 1 hour on a low heat, stirring often.

4 Add the palm sugar and fish sauce to the saucepan. Cook for 30 minutes on a low heat. Taste and adjust if necessary.

5 To store, spoon into jars, cover with oil, seal and refrigerate.

crispy-skinned, twice-cooked baby chicken with sticky black rice and chilli jam

This has been one of our menu staples since the early days of the Paragon and the demand for it remains constant. The technique for the preparation of the chickens is a classic Chinese one that results in the birds taking on the aromatic flavours of the stock and the skin developing a lacquered and crisp appearance. The flavours used in the stock are reinforced in the black rice and the Chilli Jam balances the spices and the textures, giving a hot sweetness.
The Master Stock can be used and reused, its flavour intensifying with age, so once you have made it, use it or boil it once a week and it will live on almost indefinitely. The sticky rice can be prepared in advance and reheated just before serving, if you like. To do so, spoon the cooled rice into individual oiled moulds and steam for 10 minutes.

6 × 500 g baby chickens
6 litres vegetable oil for deep-frying
1 tablespoon sea salt
2 teaspoons five-spice powder
1 teaspoon sichuan peppercorns, roasted and ground
6 teaspoons Chilli Jam (see page 34)

Master Stock
3 litres chicken stock
300 ml dark soy sauce (preferably Elephant brand)
250 ml light soy sauce
100 ml Chinese brown rice wine (shaosing)
1 small lump yellow rock sugar (about 1 tablespoon)
2 whole star anise
1 piece cassia bark
1 teaspoon fennel seeds
1 teaspoon sichuan peppercorns
1 black cardamom pod, cracked open
2 pieces dried tangerine peel
2 red bird's-eye chillies
4 slices fresh ginger
2 slices fresh galangal
3 pieces licorice root

Sticky Black Rice
1 brown onion, finely diced
2 red bird's-eye chillies, finely diced
2 cloves garlic, finely diced
1 teaspoon freshly diced ginger
50 ml vegetable oil
2 pieces dried tangerine peel, soaked and cleaned
1 teaspoon fennel seeds, roasted and ground
2 black dates, minced
250 g sticky (glutinous) black rice, washed
750 ml chicken stock
25 ml fish sauce
1 teaspoon black pepper, freshly ground

1 To make the Master Stock, bring all the ingredients to a boil in a large stockpot. Cook for 1 hour on a gentle simmer and then strain through a fine-mesh sieve. Discard the refuse and bring the Master Stock to a boil in a 10 litre stockpot.

2 Clean the chickens and remove the wings at the elbow. Dry thoroughly with a clean tea towel, inside and out.

3 Turn the stock down to a mere simmer and submerge the chickens, making sure they are completely covered. Cook the chickens for 18 minutes and remove immediately with a wire sieve, being careful not to damage the skin. At no time during this process should the stock be allowed to boil.

4 Cover a tray with a clean, dry tea towel and drain any residual stock from the chickens. Place chickens breast-side down on the tray and refrigerate overnight.

5 Make the Sticky Black Rice before finishing off the chickens (the whole process takes about 30 minutes). Fry the onion, chilli, garlic and ginger in the oil in a large saucepan until aromatic and softened. Finely mince the tangerine peel and stir into the onion mixture with the ground fennel and dates and cook for a minute or two. Add the rice and fry a little more, stirring to coat the rice in the spices and the oil.

6 Bring the chicken stock to a boil and add to the rice. Cook over a low heat until the liquid has been absorbed. The rice should be sticky but not soggy or sloppy. Stir the fish sauce and pepper into the rice and set aside.

7 Just before serving, heat the vegetable oil to 180°C in a deep-fryer or a deep saucepan. Deep-fry the chickens 2 or 3 at a time for 5 minutes, depending on the size and capacity of your deep-fryer. Drain well.

8 Remove the chickens from the oil and drain upright on paper towel to allow any oil to escape. Cut each bird into quarters and remove the backbone by cutting along either side of it. Then separate the legs from the breasts by slicing through, following the line of the leg.

9 Put the rice into the centre of each serving plate and sit the two breast pieces on either side of the rice. Place the 2 legs on top of the breasts so the bird appears to have been rejoined.

10 Mix together the sea salt, five-spice powder and the ground sichuan peppercorns and sprinkle over the meat.

11 Spoon the Chilli Jam on top of the rice and serve immediately.

Serves 6

rare kangaroo medallions with smoked eggplant, harissa and spicy masala sauce

I take my lead here from the hedonistic flavours and textures of the Middle East but give the dish a particularly Australian twist by using kangaroo meat. It is a bold combination that enlivens the palate, the components working together to make a perfect whole. I tend to use strong and complex flavours with kangaroo; it is a meat that holds its own in assertive company, its flavour not being lost in the process. Kangaroo is a beautiful meat to work with, as long as you treat it with care and don't overcook it. The dish works well, too, when lamb, beef or venison is used instead of kangaroo.

The Smoked Eggplant Purée is a variation of the well-known Lebanese baba ghannouj and has been adapted from Claudia Roden's classic New Book of Middle Eastern Food.

1 teaspoon black peppercorns, freshly ground
1 teaspoon coriander seeds, roasted and ground
6 × 150 g kangaroo striploin (sirloin, backstrap or saddle) fillets, trimmed
olive oil
vegetable oil for deep-frying
6 × 2 cm thick slices eggplant
6 teaspoons Harissa (see page 36)

Spicy Masala Sauce
2 teaspoons belacan (shrimp paste)
75 ml vegetable oil
25 ml sesame oil
1 brown onion, finely chopped
4 large cloves garlic, finely chopped
1 tablespoon freshly minced ginger
2 slices fresh galangal, finely chopped
5 red bird's-eye chillies, finely chopped
2 slices fresh turmeric, finely chopped
4 coriander roots, minced
1 teaspoon sichuan peppercorns, roasted and ground
2 teaspoons dried prawns, roasted and ground
1 teaspoon cummin seeds, roasted and ground
2 teaspoons coriander seeds, roasted and ground
1 teaspoon turmeric powder
pinch of freshly grated nutmeg
8 fresh curry leaves
1 stick cinnamon
100 ml tomato purée
150 ml coconut cream
50 g palm sugar, shaved
1.5 litres beef or veal demi-glace
25 ml fish sauce

Smoked Eggplant Purée
4 large eggplants, smoked and peeled
8 cloves garlic
2 teaspoons sea salt
180 ml tahini
120 ml lemon juice, strained
1 teaspoon cummin seeds, roasted and ground
200 ml virgin olive oil

1 To make the Spicy Masala Sauce, dry-roast the belacan in a frying pan over a medium heat.

2 Heat a large, wide-based saucepan, add the oils and fry the onion, garlic, ginger, galangal, chilli, fresh turmeric and coriander roots until the onion just begins to take on colour.

3 Add the dried prawns and spices, stirring until the mixture becomes fragrant. Stir in the tomato purée, coconut cream and palm sugar and cook on a gentle heat for a few minutes until the mixture starts to bubble.

4 Add the demi-glace to the saucepan, bring to a boil, then reduce the heat and simmer the sauce for 1 hour to reduce until the sauce coats the back of a spoon. Skim to remove any excess oil and scum. Remove from the heat, sieve to extract all juices, and discard the cooked solids. Add the fish sauce, taste and adjust the seasoning if necessary. Set aside.

5 To make the Smoked Eggplant Purée, squeeze out any liquid from the warm eggplants, then chop them. Blend the garlic with the salt in a food processor. Add the chopped eggplant and blend until smooth. Add the tahini and lemon juice alternately, pulsing between additions, and then add the cummin. With the motor still running, slowly pour in the olive oil until a smooth paste forms. Refrigerate until required.

6 To prepare the meat, mix the pepper and coriander and sprinkle over the kangaroo fillets. Brush well with olive oil.

7 Heat a heavy-based frying pan large enough to hold the fillets in a single layer until very hot. Sear the oiled meat on both sides for 2–3 minutes. Do not overcook. Rest in a warm place for 5 minutes.

8 Heat the vegetable oil in a deep-fryer and fry the eggplant rounds until golden on both sides. Drain.

9 To serve, reheat the Smoked Eggplant Purée in a steamer and bring the sauce to a boil. Check the meat; it may need to be reheated in a hot oven for 1 minute. Spoon 1½ tablespoons of the purée in the centre of each serving plate and top with a disc of fried eggplant. Cut each kangaroo fillet into 4 or 5 slices and arrange on top of the eggplant. Spoon some sauce around the purée and add a teaspoon of Harissa to the top of the meat.

Serves 6

clay pot of red emperor fillets with aromatic curry sauce and rice pilaf

This is a popular and convenient way of serving a curry at the table in an elegant manner. The fish curry is gently cooked in two clay or sand pots that are taken straight from the oven to the table. Clay pots in varying sizes can be found in Asian food stores at very reasonable prices. They need to be seasoned when new and should not be placed on a direct flame or heat. Cooking in a clay pot allows the natural juices of the food to be sealed in.

12 bok choy hearts
900 g red emperor fillets (or any other reef or white flesh fish), cleaned and trimmed
6 snake beans, cut into 3 cm lengths
coriander leaves to garnish

Curry Sauce
18 red shallots, peeled
vegetable oil
6 tablespoons Aromatic Curry Paste (see page 38)
600 ml coconut milk
600 ml fish stock
6 large red chillies, split open
12 fresh curry leaves
50 ml fish sauce
coriander leaves for garnish

Rice Pilaf
250 g basmati rice
2 brown onions
50 ml vegetable oil
3 cloves garlic
1 tablespoon ghee
1 teaspoon nigella seeds
1/2 teaspoon cardamom seeds, ground
1 bay leaf
4 whole cloves
1/2 stick cinnamon
1 litre water
25 g unsalted butter
1 1/2 teaspoons sea salt
1 teaspoon freshly ground black pepper

1 To make the Rice Pilaf, soak the rice in cold water for 1 hour, then rinse and strain.

2 Preheat the oven to 250°C. Finely slice one of the onions lengthwise. In a wide-based braising pan, cook the sliced onion in the oil until golden and slightly crispy. Drain the oil from the onion and set the onion aside.

3 Finely mince the remaining onion and the garlic and cook in the ghee until softened. Add the spices and seasoning to the onion and stir for a minute to release the flavours. Add the washed rice and the water, cover the pan with a lid and cook in the oven for 15 minutes until the rice is cooked and the liquid has been absorbed. Remove the pan from the oven and discard the bay leaf, cloves and cinnamon stick. Add the reserved crispy onion and keep warm. Turn off the oven and open the oven door to help cool it down quickly. (The clay pots need to go into a cool or cold oven in due course.)

4 To make the Curry Sauce, soften the shallots in a little oil in a frying pan over medium heat until golden. Mix the curry paste with the coconut milk and fish stock in a clean saucepan and add the cooked shallots, split chillies and curry leaves. Stir and bring to a boil. Reduce the heat and simmer, uncovered, for 20 minutes, then add the fish sauce.

5 While the sauce is simmering, bring a large saucepan of water to a boil and blanch the bok choy hearts for 1 minute only. Refresh immediately in iced water to stop the cooking and retain the colour. Drain.

6 Put the clay pots into the oven and turn up the heat as far as it will go.

7 Clean and trim the red emperor fillets and cut into 10 cm lengths (the fillets usually divide naturally into about 3 pieces). You should end up with 24 pieces of fish (4 per person) that are all about the same size, which will ensure even cooking.

8 Divide the fish fillets, snake beans and blanched bok choy hearts between the warmed clay pots and spoon the Curry Sauce over. Mix thoroughly with a spoon or pair of tongs. Cover the pots with their lids and return to the oven for 5 minutes until the fish is just cooked.

9 Just before serving, stir the butter through the rice and check the seasoning. Put the hot clay pots on underplates and carefully remove the hot lids. Sprinkle each dish with some coriander leaves and cover the pots with cool lids (so fingers don't get burnt) and take to the table. Serve the hot rice from another bowl or spoon onto serving plates.

Serves 6

duck and fennel sausage with duck livers, spiced lentils and chilli jam

Sausage-making requires time and patience, so if you have neither, buy some spicy sausages from a reliable butcher and proceed with the rest of the recipe. I have included the sausage recipe because the textures and flavours work so well together and the sausages are well worth persevering with. The ingredients will yield about 24 sausages, which need to be hung for at least three days. They will keep for up to 2 weeks in the refrigerator.

120 g red lentils
50 ml olive oil
1 brown onion, minced
3 garlic cloves, minced
3 tablespoons Spiced Tomato and Chilli Pickle (see page 39)
250 ml chicken stock
50 g unsalted butter
1 teaspoon sea salt
1 teaspoon black peppercorns, freshly ground
12 large duck livers, brushed with olive oil
3 handfuls of small spinach leaves, washed and stems removed
6 teaspoons Chilli Jam (see page 34)

Duck and Fennel Sausages

20 sausage skins (available from butchers)
1 × 1.7 kg duck
10 dried shiitake mushrooms
1 tablespoon freshly minced ginger
4 cloves garlic, minced
1 dried chipotle chilli, roasted and ground
2 teaspoons chopped garlic chives
3 tablespoons diced fennel bulb
12 water chestnuts, diced
2 coriander roots, minced
2 drops of sesame oil
2 teaspoons sea salt
1 teaspoon sichuan peppercorns, ground
1 teaspoon white peppercorns, freshly ground

1 To make the Duck and Fennel Sausages, soak the sausage skins in cold, salted water for 24 hours.

2 Remove the flesh and fat from the duck, discard the bones and skin (or keep them to make a stock), chop the meat and fat roughly and refrigerate until very cold. Pass the chilled meat and fat through a mincer on a coarse grind.

3 Soak the mushrooms in a little warm water for 30 minutes to reconstitute them. Drain and slice the mushrooms.

4 In a large bowl, mix together all the sausage ingredients except the skins until well amalgamated and evenly distributed.

5 Drain and wash the sausage skins and fill them with the prepared mixture, using a piping bag and nozzle. Do not overfill the casings or they will burst when you twist them into lengths, so leave a little slack. Twist the filled casings at 10 cm intervals, tie with a piece of string to secure and hang the sausages in the refrigerator for 3 days before using.

6 Soak the lentils for 30 minutes, then drain and wash them.

7 Heat the oil in a wide-based saucepan, add the onion and garlic and sauté until softened. Add the pickle and sauté for a minute or two, stirring, then stir in the washed lentils.

8 Pour the stock into the saucepan, bring to a boil and reduce the heat. Simmer until the liquid has been absorbed by the lentils, which should be soft by this stage. Stir in the butter, salt and pepper.

9 Grill 6 of the sausages until the skins become crisp and they are cooked through (about 5 minutes). Rest in a warm place.

10 Heat a heavy-based frying pan and, when hot, quickly sear the oiled livers on both sides, allowing them to remain quite rare. Remove from the heat.

11 To serve, slice each sausage in half on the diagonal. Stir the spinach leaves into the lentils until they begin to wilt. Spoon the lentils and spinach onto serving plates and top with a sliced sausage, livers and a teaspoonful of Chilli Jam. Serve immediately.

Serves 6

wok-seared tuna and tatsoi with lemongrass, chilli, basil and roasted peanuts

Every time this dish appears on our menu, it almost walks out the door. Make it when you can use the very best tuna in season, preferably sashimi-quality. Its firm flesh responds brilliantly to the lemongrass and chilli and the fast cooking method and with all the basic preparation being done in advance, you can pull a great trick out of your hat in the blink of an eye. As with most Chinese or Asian cooking, the time is consumed in the preparation, making the final cooking and assembly very quick and effortless.
The end result will be much better if each serve is cooked separately in a small wok as the cooking relies on using a quick, high heat to ensure that the ingredients don't stew. Small Teflon woks are available from Asian food stores. The Tamarind Dressing keeps for 3 months, refrigerated.

1 × 1 kg piece yellowfin belly tuna, uncleaned
6 tablespoons Lemongrass and Chilli Paste (see page 35)
70 ml peanut oil
20 ml sesame oil
2 small carrots, cut into julienne
1 long cucumber, shaved lengthwise
6 teaspoons holy basil leaves
12 spring onions, cut into 2 cm pieces
2 large red chillies, cut into julienne
½ daikon radish, cut into julienne
6 handfuls of tatsoi leaves
6 teaspoons raw peanuts, roasted and crushed

Tamarind Dressing
400 ml tamarind juice
60 g palm sugar, shaved
300 ml fresh lime juice, strained
50 ml ginger juice
100 ml fish sauce
50 ml sesame oil

1 Trim the tuna, removing the bloodline, and cut the fish into 2 cm square cubes (you should have about 750 g left after cleaning the fish).

2 Mix the lemongrass paste with the oils in a large bowl and add the tuna cubes. Coat well and marinate for 1–2 hours in the refrigerator.

3 While the tuna is marinating, make the Tamarind Dressing. Heat the tamarind juice with the palm sugar until the sugar has dissolved. Allow to cool.

4 Mix all the dressing ingredients together in a bowl and taste. The three prominent flavours (sweetness from the sugar, sourness from the tamarind and lime and saltiness from the fish sauce) should be in harmony. Adjust if necessary. To store, pour the dressing into jars and refrigerate.

5 Heat the woks and, when hot, add the tuna and marinating juices and toss for 1 minute over a high heat to seal. Add 360 ml of the Tamarind Dressing with the carrot, cucumber, basil, spring onion, chilli and radish and continue to toss with a pair of tongs.

6 Add the tatsoi leaves and toss once. Do not overcook. Pile the stir-fry onto serving plates, sprinkle with the crushed peanuts and serve immediately.

Serves 6

Wok-seared Tuna and Tatsoi with Lemongrass, Chilli, Basil and Roasted Peanuts

prawn and coconut laksa with prawn wontons

Laksa soups have become a perennial favourite snack or meal in everyday eating in Australia, everyone seeming to know of the best *place that makes a laksa, regardless of which city you may be in. Laksa seems to have become the most celebrated dish of Nyonya cooking and we often have our own version of the classic on the Paramount menu, its richness greatly admired and appreciated. The wontons used in this dish can be made up to 2 hours beforehand and refrigerated.*

3 tablespoons Laksa Paste (see page 37)
450 ml coconut milk
450 ml prawn stock
2 teaspoons fresh lime juice, strained
30 ml fish sauce
3 teaspoons fried shallot slices
3 teaspoons coriander leaves
3 red bird's-eye chillies, finely sliced
3 teaspoons Vietnamese mint leaves

Prawn Wontons
120 g green prawn meat, cleaned and minced
1 teaspoon freshly minced galangal
2 fresh kaffir lime leaves, finely shredded
3 teaspoons coriander leaves, chopped
½ teaspoon black peppercorns, freshly ground
18 fresh wonton skins
egg white
rice flour

1 To prepare the Prawn Wontons, mix the prawn meat, galangal, lime leaves, coriander and pepper thoroughly in a bowl.

2 Arrange the wonton skins on a flat, cool surface in a single layer and brush each one with egg white. Spoon a little of the prawn mixture onto the centre of each wonton skin and fold in half to form a triangle. Press the edges to seal. Sprinkle a tray with rice flour and transfer the wontons to it. Sprinkle the tops of the wontons with rice flour and set aside until the soup is ready.

3 To make the soup, stir the Laksa Paste into the coconut milk in a large saucepan and gently bring to a boil. Reduce the heat and simmer, uncovered, for 10 minutes.

4 Add the stock to the saucepan and bring to a boil. Reduce the heat and simmer, uncovered, for a further 15 minutes. Season with the lime juice and fish sauce. Taste and adjust if necessary.

5 Just before serving, add the wontons to the boiling soup for 2 minutes. Ladle the soup into 6 deep bowls, allowing 3 wontons per bowl and garnish with the fried shallot slices, coriander, chilli and Vietnamese mint leaves.

Serves 6

steamed snapper fillet with saffron noodles and spiced tomato chilli sauce

To eat and enjoy fish cooked in this manner is to understand the meaning of ambrosial indulgence and pleasure. Saffron has the ability to bring about such delight and, used in this context, offers a subliminal experience. Use only the freshest firm-textured fish (preferably cut from a large, deep-sea fish) for the best results. Small, thin fillets will not give a good result.

6 × 150 g thick snapper fillets
150 g saffron butter, softened
9 tablespoons Spiced Tomato and Chilli Pickle (see page 39)
9 ripe tomatoes, peeled, seeded and quartered
½ teaspoon sea salt
½ teaspoon black peppercorns, freshly ground

Saffron Noodles
½ teaspoon saffron threads
25 ml reduced tomato essence
225 g plain flour
50 g gluten flour
½ teaspoon sea salt
1 teaspoon white peppercorns, freshly ground
3 large (61 g) eggs
rice flour

1 To make the Saffron Noodles, infuse the saffron in the tomato essence over a gentle heat and allow to cool. Blend all the noodle ingredients except the rice flour in a food processor until the dough forms a ball. Refrigerate the dough, wrapped in plastic foodwrap, for 1 hour.

2 Divide the chilled dough into 6 pieces. Flatten each piece with a rolling pin and then work the dough through the rollers of a pasta machine, starting on the widest setting and working and stretching the dough each time until you reach the second-finest setting. Each time the dough passes through the rollers, sprinkle it with some rice flour to prevent it sticking. Pass each sheet of dough through the spaghetti cutters on the pasta machine. Hang the noodles over a broom handle until ready to cook.

3 Brush the snapper fillets with 60 g of the softened saffron butter.

4 Bring the pickle to a boil in a saucepan and add the tomato and remaining saffron butter. Stir over the heat until the butter has been incorporated. Season with the salt and pepper and keep warm.

5 Bring a saucepan of water to a rapid boil and cook the noodles for 2 minutes, then strain.

6 Grill the snapper fillets for 5–6 minutes depending on their thickness. Be careful not to overcook them.

7 Spoon the tomato sauce onto 6 serving plates, make a nest of saffron noodles in the centre of the sauce puddle and sit the grilled fish on top of the noodles. The fish should be glistening and a rich yellow from the saffron.

Serves 6

Pickled Ginger

Green or young ginger is an integral ingredient in our cooking at the Paramount, invaluable because it gives a spiciness and freshness to prepared foods. It aids digestion, cutting the richness and fattiness of particular dishes, and has a distinctive flavour and aroma that cannot be substituted by any other ingredient. A rhizome that grows on an underground stem just as turmeric and galangal do, ginger is used prolifically in food preparations of Asian origin and particularly in China where it is used in abundance. It is used medicinally as well as in cooking and acts as a preservative and a warming and clarifying agent.

Pickled ginger is a staple of Japanese cooking. Young ginger roots are preserved in a vinegar solution and used as a seasoning and a condiment, traditionally with grilled meats, sashimi and sushi. When we pickle ginger for use in the Restaurant and the Store, we choose ginger that is green. It has been picked at a young age and has not been left in cold storage or allowed to mature: the skin is smooth, translucent and soft and needs little or no peeling, the flesh is firm but not fibrous and the tips have a pink blush. The ginger is cut into tissue-thin slices and covered with a vinegar solution. It is an ingredient I always have on hand to toss into seafood salads, add to stir-fries, sprinkle over fried spring rolls or fish cakes, or as an addition to a plate of thinly sliced raw fish and seafood. The effect of pickling mellows the flavour of the ginger, which gives a refreshing and gentle lift to the ingredients it accompanies.

pickled ginger

Ready for use a few days after pickling, Pickled Ginger keeps for a lengthy time, refrigerated.

300 g green ginger knobs, peeled and trimmed
350 ml rice vinegar
50 ml fresh lime juice, strained
25 ml fish sauce

1 Cut the ginger into extremely fine slices, using either a sharp knife with a fine blade, a mandolin or a sharp, thin-bladed cleaver.

2 Mix the rice vinegar, lime juice and fish sauce together in a jug. Pack the sliced ginger into sterilised jars, cover with the vinegar and mix well. Seal and refrigerate until ready to use.

tea and spice smoked quail with pickled cucumber and ginger

The smoking mixture used in this recipe imparts wonderful aromas to the meat but the kitchen tends to reek afterwards, so keep the window open and the fan on! The quantity given here is sufficient for two 'smokes' and the mixture seems to keep forever.

6 large quails
1 teaspoon five-spice powder
1 teaspoon sea salt
$\frac{1}{2}$ teaspoon sichuan peppercorns, roasted and ground
2 small eggplants, smoked, peeled and sliced
2 continental cucumbers
1 tablespoon finely diced red onion
2 tablespoons Pickled Ginger, cut into julienne (see page 52)
2 teaspoons purple basil leaves, finely sliced
2 red radish, cut into julienne
24 small radicchio leaves

Tea and Spice Smoking Mixture
1 tablespoon oolong tea leaves
1 tablespoon jasmine tea
zest of 1 orange
2 pieces dried tangerine peel, broken up
2 tablespoons jasmine rice
2 tablespoons brown sugar
3 whole star anise
2 teaspoons sichuan peppercorns
3 pieces cassia bark

Sweet and Sour Dressing
100 ml vegetable oil
2 red bird's-eye chillies, chopped
2 small cloves garlic, finely sliced
60 ml light soy sauce
100 ml cider vinegar
150 ml sugar syrup

1 Clean the quails and, using a sharp knife, split each one open down the backbone. Flatten the quails and arrange on a tray, skin-side up.

2 Mix together the five-spice powder, sea salt and ground sichuan pepper. Sprinkle this mixture over the quails, cover and cure for 3 hours in the refrigerator. Allow the quails to come back to room temperature before smoking, otherwise the smoking time will be affected.

3 While the quails are curing, make the Tea and Spice Smoking Mixture by combining all the ingredients. Store at room temperature in an airtight container.

4 To make the Sweet and Sour Dressing, heat the oil in a saucepan with the chilli and garlic over a low heat until the garlic becomes golden but does not burn. Add the soy sauce, vinegar and sugar syrup and bring to a boil. Remove from the heat, allow to cool, then strain and store in the refrigerator until ready to use.

5 To smoke the quails, line a large wok with foil. Put a strip of baking paper down the middle of a metal steamer tray that fits neatly over the wok. Be sure to leave some gaps along the sides of the tray when putting in the paper or the smoking will not be as effective.

6 Put the foil-lined wok, without the steamer tray in position, over a high flame or heat. Arrange the quails skin-side up on the baking paper in the steamer tray, making sure they do not overlap (it may be necessary to do this in 2 batches to ensure even smoking).

7 Sprinkle 4 tablespoons of the smoking mixture over the base of the hot wok and, when it starts to smoke seriously and burn at the edges, place the steamer tray with the quails over it and cover the wok with a tight-fitting lid. Use foil to secure the lid further, if necessary. (This must be done under an effective exhaust vent or you will smoke and smell out your kitchen.)

8 Smoke the quails for 6 minutes. Remove the steamer tray immediately, fold the burnt foil over on itself and discard outside straight away. (Throw these burnt offerings in the bin when they have cooled down.) Take the quails out of the steamer and allow to cool.

9 Remove the breast meat from the quails, then take the leg meat off the bone and discard the carcasses. Slice the breasts and the leg meat in two.

10 Warm the Sweet and Sour Dressing over a gentle heat. Put the quail meat into half the dressing with the smoked eggplant and marinate for 3 minutes.

11 Using a vegetable peeler, peel the cucumbers and shave into long strips, discarding the skin and the core of seeds. Pickle the cucumber shavings in the remaining dressing in a large bowl for 3 minutes only (any longer and the cucumber will start to disintegrate).

12 Add the remaining ingredients to the cucumber with the quail and eggplant and mix thoroughly to ensure even distribution. Pile carefully onto serving plates and serve immediately.

Serves 6

steamed custards of yabbies, shiitake mushrooms and ginger

These custards are an adaptation of the delicate Japanese chawan-mushi savoury custards that make a perfectly light start to a meal. Don't expect the custards to set firm as the liquid dispelled from the ingredients during the cooking will give the custards a generous wobble and, when the surface is broken with eating, the custard will take on a soupy appearance, which is why they are served in the bowls in which they are steamed. Experiment with other ingredients and come up with your own combinations, remembering these custards are a delicate treat and therefore ingredients with subtle flavours work best.

1.5 litres fish stock
12 green yabbies in their shells
30 ml tomato essence
30 ml mirin
6 fresh shiitake mushrooms, each cut into 5 strips
3 teaspoons Pickled Ginger, cut into julienne (see page 52)
6 teaspoons finely sliced spring onions
2 teaspoons coriander leaves
6 large (61 g) eggs
3 drops chilli oil

1 Put the fish stock in a stockpot and bring to a boil over a high heat. Add the yabbies and reduce the heat to medium, so the stock just bubbles. Cook the yabbies for 2 minutes only, just enough to loosen the flesh from their shells.

2 Remove the yabbies from the stock and plunge into icy water to stop the cooking. Remove the meat from the yabbies, devein the tails and set aside until ready to use. Add the yabby shells to the stock and simmer for 30 minutes.

3 Strain the stock through a fine-mesh sieve or piece of muslin and measure out 900 ml (reserve the remaining stock for later use). Return the 900 ml stock to the heat in a clean saucepan, add the tomato essence and the mirin and simmer for 5 minutes. Remove from the heat and allow to cool.

4 Bring a large saucepan of water to a gentle boil.

5 Arrange 6 small Japanese or Chinese round-based bowls on a metal steamer tray that will fit snugly over the saucepan of boiling water. To each bowl add 2 yabby tails, 5 slices of mushroom, 1/2 teaspoon of ginger, 1 teaspoon of sliced spring onions and a few coriander leaves.

6 Gently whisk together the eggs, chilli oil and 960 ml of the reserved stock without aerating the mixture and pour carefully over the ingredients in the bowls.

7 Place the steamer tray over the saucepan of gently boiling water and cover with a tight-fitting lid. Reduce the heat to low so the water is just simmering (any more than this and the custards will separate). Steam for 20 minutes or until the custards have just set and still have a slight wobble in the centre.

8 Remove the steamer from the heat and carefully take out the bowls of custard. Serve immediately with each bowl on a flat underplate with a napkin between the two to prevent sliding.

Serves 6

seared beef fillet with lemongrass, ginger and pickled green papaya

A refreshing and easy warm salad to make, with great flavours that tingle the palate. Serve as an entrée or as part of a combination of dishes served together. The Pickled Green Papaya will keep, refrigerated, for 1 month.

500 g beef eye fillet, trimmed
30 ml vegetable oil
200 ml Tamarind Dressing (see page 44)
1 stalk lemongrass, finely minced
1 red bird's-eye chilli, minced
2 coriander roots, finely minced
2 fresh kaffir lime leaves, finely shredded
zest of 1 lime
2 teaspoons minced galangal
1 teaspoon minced ginger
1 teaspoon dried shrimp, roasted and ground
1 teaspoon jasmine rice, roasted and ground
1 teaspoon sesame seeds

Pickled Ginger Salad
6 teaspoons pickled ginger, drained
6 cm daikon radish, peeled and finely shredded
½ cucumber, peeled, seeded and finely sliced lengthwise
12 red shallots finely sliced
1 tablespoon finely shredded Vietnamese mint leaves
2 cups watercress leaves

Pickled Green Papaya
1 small green papaya
100 ml fresh lime juice, strained
80 ml fish sauce
60 g palm sugar, shaved
1 red bird's-eye chilli, minced

1 To make the Pickled Green Papaya, wash the papaya and quarter it lengthwise. Remove the seeds and slice very finely using a mandolin or slicer. Mix the rest of the ingredients together and add the sliced papaya. Allow to pickle for at least 3 days before using.

2 Brush the beef fillet with the oil and sear on all sides very quickly in a hot pan over high heat, ensuring that the meat remains very rare in the middle. Remove from the pan and rest in a warm place for 10 minutes.

3 In a large bowl, mix together the remaining ingredients. Rest the beef fillet in the dressing for 5 minutes, turning once.

4 In another bowl, mix together the salad ingredients.

5 Slice the beef into 1 cm thick slices and mix with the salad. Add enough dressing to wet the ingredients without drowning them and pile onto 6 serving plates. Top with some slices of the Pickled Green Papaya and add a little extra dressing if necessary. Serve immediately.

Serves 6

blue swimmer crab, shaved coconut and mint salad with fried shallots

This dish, with its clean and refreshing flavours, is the perfect summer salad or light entrée for a lunch or dinner and a must for when the crabs are at their best. While I recommend using blue swimmer crabs here, it also works very well with mudcrabs. Its success lies in everything being absolutely fresh and very fine knife work, so that the flavours and textures work harmoniously together. The Coconut Dressing keeps well for a week, refrigerated.

6 uncooked blue swimmer crabs (to yield 500 g crab meat)
3 tablespoons finely shaved fresh coconut flesh
6 spring onions, finely sliced
1 large red chilli, seeded and very finely sliced
1 tablespoon Pickled Ginger, cut into julienne (see page 52)
½ cucumber, seeded and cut into julienne
1 tablespoon mint leaves, finely shredded
2 tablespoons Vietnamese mint leaves, finely shredded
1 tablespoon coriander leaves
3 teaspoons finely sliced red shallots
8 fresh kaffir lime leaves, very finely shredded
2 handfuls of mitsuba leaves, washed
betel or banana leaves for serving (optional)
6 teaspoons fried shallot slices

Coconut Lime Dressing
100 ml fresh lime juice, strained
100 ml coconut vinegar
25 ml fish sauce
25 ml sugar syrup
2 pinches of freshly ground black pepper
3 drops sesame oil
25 ml olive oil

1 To make the Coconut Lime Dressing, whisk the ingredients together in a bowl. Taste for seasoning and adjust if necessary. Refrigerate in a sealed container until ready to use.

2 Fill a stockpot large enough to fit the crabs with water and bring to a boil. When the water reaches a rolling boil, add the crabs and cook for 6 minutes (10 minutes if using mudcrabs). Remove the crabs from the water and immediately plunge them into icy-cold water to prevent further cooking. Remove the flesh from the crabs and discard the shells (or reserve them to make a crab stock for later use). Ensure that the crab meat is free of any hard membrane and shell.

3 In a large bowl, mix together the crab meat, coconut, spring onion, chilli, ginger, cucumber, mints, coriander, red shallots and lime leaves. Pour in the dressing and allow to stand for 3 minutes only, just long enough for the flavours to mingle.

4 Dry the mitsuba leaves thoroughly. Toss the leaves in the dressed crab and mix carefully.

5 If desired, arrange betel leaves or a round of banana leaf on each serving plate. Pile the salad onto the plates and sprinkle over the fried shallot slices. Serve immediately.

Serves 6

Blue Swimmer Crab, Shaved Coconut and Mint Salad with Fried Shallots

Mustard and Horseradish Pastes

Horseradish and mustard are two of the world's strongest and most evocative tastes, ones that are acquired and usually associated with the adult palate rather than infant or adolescent desires. Both are members of the cabbage family but infinitely more challenging than the common garden-variety cabbage.

Horseradish grows as a long, cylindrical root and has an appearance similar to parsnip, with a brownish skin and creamy-white, firm flesh. Its flavour is hot and pungent. Historically, it appears that horseradish was used for medicinal purposes long before it was held in any culinary regard. It has been referred to as having warming and cleansing properties as well as being an appetite enhancer. Today, it can be found in many cuisines of the world as it grows easily everywhere, particularly near the sea.

Prepared horseradish does not have the invigorating quality of fresh horseradish, which becomes quite apparent when peeling and grating the root. It is worth the effort of seeking out a supply of fresh horseradish if you find yourself addicted to the taste, or if you are a purist at heart. Select roots that are straight, dry and hard and keep them in plastic in a cool, dry place for up to a month. Horseradish loses its sharpness and pungency as soon as heat is applied, so for maximum flavour and benefit it is added to hot food at the last minute or mixed with either vinegar or sour cream to disguise its potency. Grated finely and mixed with a little wine vinegar, horseradish also preserves well.

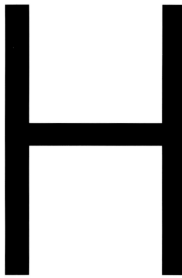

Once a year, mustard plants yield brown, black or white seeds, depending on the variety. The black seeds are the hottest and not commonly available as they need to be harvested by hand. The brown seeds are larger and milder than the black and the white seeds, which in fact are pale-yellow, are the seeds most readily available on the market and commonly used in mustard preparations. Dijon in France is noted for its unparalleled production and preparation of mustard. It is a condiment in its own right, aids digestion and is similar to horseradish in that it has a distinctive, sharp and pungent flavour that dissipates when applied to high heat. Mustard is a natural thickening or binding agent but does not respond well to boiling as it tends to separate, so when adding it to a sauce, watch it carefully. There are many varieties available – French, English, German, American, smooth, seeded and flavoured – so use a mustard that is appropriate for what you are serving. Mustard, whatever variety, is very versatile as a flavour enhancer and is a necessity for any kitchen.

At the Store we always stock a few items based on mustard or horseradish, pastes that can enliven a basic food item and make the cooking process a quick and painless operation when time is of the essence and flavour is essential. The base recipes in this chapter are also in constant use in the Restaurant in many of our preparations, due to the strength of flavour and complexity they offer.

garlic and mustard marinade paste

This paste enriches the flavour of any meat marinated in it. It can also be used to coat poultry or oily fish that is to be barbecued; mixed with a stuffing to give a more complex flavour; added to a dressing for a warm potato salad, or cooked into a basic cream sauce to serve with chicken or white-fleshed fish. It will keep for up to 3 weeks in the refrigerator.

10 large cloves garlic, minced
3 tablespoons smooth Dijon mustard
5 tablespoons thyme leaves
2½ teaspoons freshly ground black pepper
125 ml lemon juice, strained
150 ml olive oil

Put all the ingredients except the oil in a food processor and pulse to a paste. With the motor still running, drizzle the oil in gradually and process until smooth. Put the paste into a container, seal and refrigerate until required.

horseradish cream

This luscious cream is a great one to keep on hand for giving snacks a lift. It makes grilled meat or sausages more appealing and is wonderful spooned onto scrambled eggs with smoked salmon or used to spike a savoury tart. It keeps for a week refrigerated and is best made several hours ahead.

3 tablespoons crème fraîche or sour cream
1 tablespoon finely grated fresh horseradish
½ teaspoon freshly ground white pepper
2 teaspoons finely chopped chives

Gently mix all the ingredients together in a bowl with a spoon. Keep refrigerated in an airtight container until ready to use.

mustard and horseradish relish

The headiness and pungency of mustard and horseradish sit well together and make this relish a great accompaniment to cold meats, smoked fish, root vegetables, cooked offal (such as liver, brains or sweetbreads) and a charcuterie plate. It will keep, refrigerated, for 2 weeks.

2 tablespoons seeded Dijon mustard
1 tablespoon hot smooth mustard
1 tablespoon freshly grated horseradish
2 teaspoons castor sugar
1 teaspoon white peppercorns, freshly ground
2 tablespoons tiny capers, washed
3 teaspoons tarragon leaves
5 tablespoons Aïoli (see page 76)

Mix together all the ingredients except the Aïoli. Stir this mixture into the Aïoli. The relish should be quite firm with enough body to hold its own weight. To store, spoon into a container, seal and refrigerate.

smoked salmon with potato pikelet, nori omelette and horseradish cream

This dish has been with us since our days at the Paragon and the combination of flavours is a perennial favourite. The effect of stacking one layer upon another gives it a spectacular appearance, demanding that it be noticed and tasted immediately. The Pikelet Mix lasts for about 5 hours before it starts to oxidise, so don't make it too far in advance.

12 slices smoked salmon
6 teaspoons Horseradish Cream (see page 63)
2 teaspoons chopped chives
3 teaspoons fresh salmon roe

Pikelet Mix
350 g waxy potatoes, peeled and chopped
2 teaspoons chopped chives
1 large (61 g) egg
1 tablespoon plain flour
1 teaspoon freshly grated horseradish
1 teaspoon wasabi powder
1 teaspoon sea salt
½ teaspoon freshly ground black pepper
50 ml thick (45%) cream

Nori Omelettes
12 large (61 g) eggs
pinch of sea salt
½ teaspoon black pepper, freshly ground
1 teaspoon sesame oil
1 teaspoon fish sauce
2 nori seaweed sheets, toasted
vegetable oil

1 Make the Pikelet Mix by briefly blending all the ingredients except the cream in a food processor. Add the cream and pulse until just incorporated. Pour the mixture into a plastic jug, cover and refrigerate until ready to use.

2 To make the Nori Omelettes, whisk the eggs until light but not aerated and season with the salt, pepper, sesame oil and fish sauce. Cut the nori into short strips and stir into the egg mixture.

3 Heat a 20 cm Teflon frying pan and brush lightly with oil. Ladle in 40 ml of the egg mixture and spread thinly over the pan as you would a crêpe. Cook until just set and turn out onto a clean tea towel. Continue the process with the remaining mixture, stacking the omelettes on top of each other.

4 Roll up each omelette into a roulade, then wrap firmly in plastic foodwrap, securing the ends to keep the shape firm and intact. Allow to cool for 30 minutes before slicing.

5 To cook the pikelets, heat a Teflon frying pan and oil it lightly. Pour the Pikelet Mix into 6 oiled egg rings (you may need to do 3 at a time, depending on the size of your pan). Cook over a medium heat until bubbles start to appear in the batter. Flip the pikelets over to cook on the other side.

6 To assemble, cut the rolled omelettes into 1.5 cm thick slices (you will need 6 slices). Place a hot pikelet in the centre of each serving plate and top with an omelette slice. Add 2 slices of the smoked salmon, rolled into a rosette, if you desire, per plate, then a teaspoon of the Horseradish Cream and sprinkle with chives and salmon roe. Serve immediately.

Serves 6

rare venison pepper steak with glazed beetroots and horseradish cream

This dish is so vibrant, it almost speaks to you. Venison is one of those meats best cooked and eaten rare if you are to appreciate its flavour and texture. Because it has no fat, like kangaroo, it quickly becomes tough and chewy if it is overcooked or not rested properly, losing its tenderness and moisture. As it is an expensive cut of meat, treat it with the respect it deserves. The flavour of the meat is highlighted by the strength of the beetroot and horseradish, a harmonious combination. You may want to turn your oven up high just before serving in case the venison needs to be reheated for a minute or two. This recipe makes twice as much Pepper Glaze as required; the remainder can be frozen.

3 teaspoons cracked black pepper
6 × 175 g venison medallions, cut from the trimmed striploin (sirloin, backstrap or saddle) fillet
18 small beetroots, trimmed and peeled
50 g unsalted butter
50 ml olive oil
pinch of sea salt
pinch of black pepper, freshly ground
a little extra olive oil
2 teaspoons freshly grated horseradish
6 teaspoons Horseradish Cream (see page 63)

Pepper Glaze
1 brown onion, chopped
3 large cloves garlic, sliced
3 sprigs of fresh thyme
1 tablespoon black peppercorns
½ tablespoon sichuan peppercorns
100 ml brandy
200 ml red wine (preferably shiraz)
2 litres veal or beef demi-glace

Beetroot Purée
50 g unsalted butter
6 beetroots, peeled and sliced
2 small waxy potatoes, peeled and sliced
75 ml thick (45%) cream
½ teaspoon sea salt
½ teaspoon black peppercorns, freshly ground

1 To make the Pepper Glaze, heat a large stockpot, brush it with a film of oil and fry the onion, garlic, thyme and peppercorns until the onion has softened and the mixture is fragrant. Add the brandy and flame it, then add the red wine. Cook until reduced by a third and then add the demi-glace.

2 Bring the glaze to a boil and then reduce the heat. Simmer for 1 hour until reduced by half. Skim the surface occasionally to remove any scum and keep the glaze clear.

3 Pass the glaze through a conical sieve and then a fine-mesh sieve to remove all sediment and coarse particles. Taste and add some ground black pepper if necessary. Set aside until ready to use.

4 To make the Beetroot Purée, preheat the oven to 200°C and grease a gratin dish generously with most of the butter. Add the sliced beetroot and potato in layers and dot with the remaining butter. Pour over the cream and season with salt and pepper. Cover with foil and bake for 30 minutes or until the beetroot is soft when tested with a skewer. Purée the beetroot and potato in a food processor and then transfer to a blender and purée again until very fine. Taste for seasoning and adjust if necessary. Set aside.

5 Cut the beetroots into quarters lengthwise. Heat the butter and oil in a frying pan and, when foaming, add the beetroot slices and toss to coat. Cook on a low heat, stirring regularly, until the beetroots have softened and become glazed. Season with salt and pepper and set aside until ready to serve.

6 Sprinkle the cracked black pepper evenly over both sides of the venison medallions. Heat a heavy-based frying pan until very hot. Add a splash of olive oil and immediately toss in the peppered venison and seal for 2 minutes per side. Rest the meat in a warm place for 10 minutes.

7 While the meat is resting, gently reheat the Beetroot Purée in a steamer and bring the Pepper Glaze to a boil in a saucepan. Add the glazed beetroot slices to the sauce and simmer for 5 minutes. Stir the grated horseradish into the sauce just before serving.

8 To serve, put the meat into a hot oven for 1–2 minutes, if necessary. Spoon the purée onto the centre of 6 serving plates, cut each piece of venison into 4 thick slices and lay on top of the purée and arrange the beetroots and sauce around the meat. Add a teaspoonful of Horseradish Cream to the meat and serve immediately.

Serves 6

Rare Venison Pepper Steak with Glazed Beetroots and Horseradish Cream

mudcrab omelette with horseradish cream and caviar

This is food for the gods, an ethereal taste sensation created by a combination of flavours: the sweetness of the crab meat, the iodine saltiness of the caviar and the creaminess of the omelette and the horseradish cream. Make it with tender, loving care and your pains will be rewarded with heavenly applause and lip-smacking responses. The omelettes work best if made individually, so have on hand a couple of small 15 cm Teflon omelette or frying pans to cook two at a time.

2 × 1 kg uncooked mudcrabs
12 large (61 g) eggs
a few drops of sesame oil
25 ml mirin
25 ml fish sauce
3 teaspoons freshly chopped chives
2 pinches of freshly ground white pepper
60 g unsalted butter
6 teaspoons Horseradish Cream (see page 63)
6 teaspoons osietra or sevruga caviar
virgin olive oil
extra chives for garnish

1 Bring a large saucepan of water to a rolling boil, add the crabs and cook for 6 minutes. The shells will go red during the cooking process and the meat will be easier to remove from the shell. Remove the crabs from the saucepan and immerse in icy-cold water to stop the cooking process. When the crabs have cooled enough to handle, take out of the water and remove the meat. (Keep the shells to make a stock for a soup base, if desired.)

2 Lightly whisk the eggs in a bowl and stir in the sesame oil, mirin, fish sauce, chives and pepper.

3 To make the omelette, heat two 15 cm Teflon frying pans until warm and preheat the griller of your stove. Add a teaspoon of butter to each pan and, as it melts, pour in enough omelette mixture to coat the base generously. As the omelette begins to set on the bottom, sprinkle on some crab meat so it cooks into the soft egg. Flash the pans under the heated griller for a few seconds to seal the top of the omelettes and immediately turn out onto serving plates. Fold the omelettes over in the middle, being careful not to crack them. Rest the cooked omelettes in a warm place (but not the oven) while cooking the remaining serves. (The cooking process is so quick the omelettes should stay hot until being taken to the table.)

4 Top each omelette with a teaspoon each of Horseradish Cream and caviar, drizzle very lightly with virgin olive oil, sprinkle over a few snipped chives and serve.

Serves 6

milk-fed veal tenderloin with pancetta, creamed parsnips and mustard sauce

Make this dish with the best veal you can lay your hands on; the result will be far superior than if made with yearling beef, which is commonly passed off as veal. The tender age of milk-fed or suckling veal gives it a sublime, buttery and melt-in-the-mouth texture, a quality that cannot be matched. The silkiness of the parsnip cream matches the veal beautifully, as well as blending in with and highlighting the pungency of the mustard.

6 × 150 g veal tenderloin fillets, trimmed
30 thin slices pancetta
50 g unsalted butter
1 kg parsnips, peeled and sliced
175 ml thick (45%) cream
½ teaspoon sea salt
½ teaspoon white peppercorns, freshly ground
2 extra parsnips for chips (optional)
vegetable oil for deep-frying (optional)
2 tablespoons smooth Dijon mustard
200 ml Pepper Glaze (see page 66)

1 Preheat the oven to 180°C. Wrap each piece of veal fillet with five slices of pancetta and set aside.

2 Grease a deep-sided baking dish with most of the butter, add the sliced parsnips and stir in 75 ml of the thick cream and the remaining butter. Sprinkle with salt and pepper, cover with foil and bake for 30 minutes or until the parsnips are cooked when tested with a skewer.

3 Blend the baked parsnip in a food processor to make a thick, smooth cream. Set aside until ready to use. To reheat, spoon the parsnip cream into a baking dish, cover with foil and gently warm in a low oven so the cream does not burn. Remove from the oven and turn the temperature up high (you do this in case the meat needs reheating just before serving).

4 To make parsnip chips, use a vegetable peeler to shave the parsnips lengthwise. Heat the oil in a deep-fryer or deep saucepan and fry the shaved parsnip until crisp but not coloured. Drain on paper towels.

5 Heat a cast-iron or heavy-based frying pan, add a drizzle of oil to prevent the meat from sticking and seal the prepared fillets on all sides. This should take 5–6 minutes, by which time the pancetta will have started to crisp. Allow the meat to rest in a warm place for 8 minutes.

6 Whisk the mustard into the remaining 100 ml of thick cream. Bring the Pepper Glaze to a boil in a saucepan and stir in the mustard cream. Allow the sauce to come back to a boil to incorporate the cream and then remove from the heat.

7 Reheat the veal in the hot oven for 1 minute, if necessary, and then slice each fillet into 3 medallions. Spoon the parsnip cream onto the centre of 6 serving plates and top with the meat. Spoon the sauce around the meat and add some deep-fried parsnip chips, if using.

Serves 6

roasted corn-fed chicken with garlic mustard crust and steamed mustard greens

This dish is a tribute to the quality of the chickens bred by Glenloth Farm at Wycheproof, Victoria, giving us poultry as it should taste, not the battery-hen variety made tasteless and boring by conditions not designed for a quality product. Ask for corn-fed chickens from your supplier and take your tastebuds to new heights. The marinade paste makes this an interesting alternative to the usual roast chicken as it forms a tasty crust, sealing the juices in the meat.

180 g breadcrumbs (made from day-old, crusty white bread)
3 large (61 g) eggs, beaten
6 tablespoons Garlic and Mustard Marinade Paste (see page 62)
6 teaspoons brown mustard seeds
3 × 900 g corn-fed chickens
12 cloves garlic
6 sprigs of thyme
1 teaspoon sea salt
1 teaspoon black peppercorns, freshly ground
100 ml olive oil
150 g mustard greens, washed

1 Preheat the oven to 250°C. In a large bowl, mix together the breadcrumbs, eggs, marinade paste and mustard seeds until well incorporated.

2 Wipe the chickens inside and out with a clean, dry tea towel. Place 4 garlic cloves and 2 sprigs of thyme into the cavity of each bird, and season with salt and pepper.

3 Pack the mustard crust liberally onto the outside of the birds, covering their entire surface, and truss with either a skewer or string. Put the birds in an oiled baking dish and bake for 25 minutes or until cooked. Test with a skewer, piercing the flesh near the leg joint; if the juices are clear with a touch of pink, the chicken is ready. Take the chickens out of the oven and rest in a warm place for 5 minutes.

4 Heat the olive oil in a frying pan until warm. Add the mustard greens, cover immediately with a lid and toss over a medium heat until the greens are wilted but not coloured. Season with salt and pepper and arrange on 6 serving plates.

5 Divide each chicken in two by slicing down the breastbone and backbone, then carve each half in two, separating the leg from the breast. Sit a chicken leg and breast on top of the mustard greens on each plate and pour over any excess pan juices.

Serves 6

seared beef fillet with celeriac and mustard and horseradish relish

This is a celebration of the wonderful celeriac, a root vegetable available during the colder months of the year. It is commonly used in European cooking, particularly French, and has a creamy-coloured flesh that tastes like a celery-flavoured potato. The celeriac harmonises perfectly with the Mustard and Horseradish Relish, so make the most of it when it is in season.

1 × 1.5 kg beef fillet, trimmed
25 ml olive oil
2 teaspoons cracked black pepper
2 heads of celeriac
6 tablespoons Mustard and Horseradish Relish (see page 64)

1 Preheat the oven as high as it will go.

2 Brush the fillet with the oil and sprinkle with the cracked pepper. Bake the beef in a baking dish for 8 minutes. Turn the fillet over and cook a further 5 minutes. The meat should be quite rare. Take the meat out of the oven and rest in a warm place for 10 minutes to allow the juices to settle.

3 Peel the celeriac, then grate it into a bowl of acidulated water to prevent it from discolouring.

4 Bring a saucepan of water to a boil. Take the grated celeriac out of the acidulated water and blanch for 30 seconds in the boiling water. Remove the celeriac with a sieve and run cold water over it to stop the cooking. Drain the celeriac, put it into a bowl and allow to cool. Stir the relish into the cooled celeriac.

5 Cut the hot beef fillet into 1 cm thick slices. Spoon the celeriac on to 6 serving plates. Place the sliced beef on top of the celeriac and serve.

Serves 6

Aïoli

Aïoli, a luscious amalgamation of garlic, egg yolks and olive oil, has its origins in Provençe in the south of France. Essentially a mayonnaise heavily spiked with crushed garlic, it can be served simply with grilled or barbecued fish or meat, stirred at the last minute into a vegetable soup to give it a creamy lift, added to a fish stew as in the French classic *bourride*, spread on sandwiches with cured or smoked meats or spooned onto fried sardines, taken to a picnic and added to a salad at the last minute or served with prepared salt cod, crudités or vegetables. The diversity of its use is a celebration of garlic, an ingredient around which festivals are based.

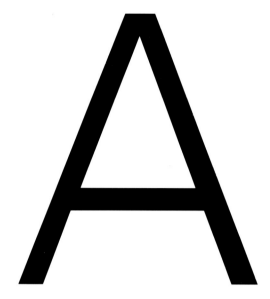

At the Restaurant, we make aïoli in two different ways. One uses freshly crushed garlic which gives a powerful blast to the palate since the garlic is digested raw. The second involves roasting a head of garlic wrapped in foil in the oven until it softens; the roasted garlic is squeezed into the emulsion, giving it a gentle and well-rounded taste. Which is chosen simply depends on the context of the dish and the preferred style. With the addition of some diced roasted red capsicum and a couple of red chillies, you have a more fiery mayonnaise known as rouille. Hailing from Marseilles, in the south of France also, it is traditionally added to bouillabaisse, a fish soup or stew; some of the stock is often used to flavour the mayonnaise.

With all mayonnaise preparations, be careful to add the oil in a thin, steady stream to ensure the emulsion thickens properly and does not separate.

aïoli

It is the emulsion of egg yolks enriched with juicy young garlic that gives Aïoli its distinctive character and taste. Like any other mayonnaise preparation, it keeps for approximately 1 week, refrigerated, in a sealed container.

6 fresh cloves garlic
2 pinches of sea salt
25 ml lemon juice, strained
25 ml white wine vinegar
3 pinches of freshly ground white pepper
2 egg yolks
250 ml virgin olive oil
250 ml vegetable oil

1 Crush the garlic with the salt in a mortar and pestle to release the aroma and flavour the salt.

2 Blend the garlic and salt in a food processor with the lemon juice, vinegar, pepper and egg yolks until well incorporated.

3 With the motor running, slowly drizzle in the combined oils in a thin, steady stream until incorporated and the mayonnaise has become thick.

4 To store, spoon the mayonnaise into a container, seal and refrigerate.

roasted garlic aïoli

This recipe requires roasted garlic but is otherwise made the same way as Aïoli. It keeps for up to 1 week, refrigerated.

1 head of garlic
2 pinches of sea salt
25 ml lemon juice, strained
25 ml white wine vinegar
3 pinches of freshly ground white pepper
2 egg yolks
250 ml virgin olive oil
250 ml vegetable oil

1 Preheat the oven to 180°C and wrap the head of garlic in foil. Bake the garlic for 30 minutes or until soft.

2 Squeeze out the soft garlic cloves and mix with the salt in a mortar and pestle.

3 Blend the garlic and salt in a food processor with the lemon juice, vinegar, pepper and egg yolks until well incorporated.

4 With the motor running, slowly drizzle in the combined oils in a thin, steady stream until incorporated and the mayonnaise has become thick.

5 To store, spoon the mayonnaise into a container, seal and refrigerate.

rouille

Add chilli and capsicum as you make Aïoli *(see page 76)* *for a more fiery alternative.*

1 quantity of Aïoli (see page 76)
1 red capsicum, roasted, peeled and chopped
2 bird's-eye chillies, seeded and minced

Make the Aïoli as directed, adding the minced chilli and chopped capsicum to the food processor with the eggs.

snapper and tomato soup with duck-egg pasta and roasted garlic aïoli

The success of this soup relies on using a good, clear, jellied snapper stock as a base. You need to procure a couple of fresh snapper heads to achieve the best results. Aïoli, by its very nature, lends itself to those flavours we associate with the Mediterranean. The Duck-egg Pasta gives the soup an added richness.

30 ml olive oil
1 brown onion, finely chopped
3 cloves garlic, finely chopped
1/2 small bulb fennel, finely chopped
10 tomatoes, roasted
150 ml tomato purée
100 ml white wine
1 litre fish stock (made with snapper bones)
1 teaspoon sea salt
1 teaspoon black peppercorns, freshly ground
300 g snapper fillet, skin on
2 tablespoons diced tomato
12 flat parsley leaves, finely shredded
6 teaspoons Roasted Garlic Aïoli (see page 77)

Duck-egg Pasta
200 g plain flour
50 g gluten flour
1/2 teaspoon sea salt
2 large duck eggs
20 ml olive oil
rice flour

1 To make the Duck-egg Pasta, sieve the flours and add to the bowl of a food processor with the salt.

2 Lightly beat the eggs and the oil, and pour into the food processor with the motor running until the dough forms a ball. Wrap the dough in plastic foodwrap and refrigerate for 2 hours.

3 Cut the dough into 5 pieces. Flatten each piece with a rolling pin on a surface lightly dusted with rice flour so that the dough will pass easily through the rollers of the pasta machine. Pass each piece of dough through the rollers of the pasta machine, starting at the widest setting and working the dough through to the thinnest setting, dusting each time with some rice flour.

4 Pass each piece of worked dough through the tagliatelle cutters of the pasta machine or, alternatively, cut the dough into strips with a sharp knife. Hang the pasta over a broom handle to dry for 30 minutes.

5 To prepare the soup, heat a large saucepan or stockpot, add the oil and gently sauté the onion, garlic and fennel until aromatic and softened. Add the roasted tomatoes and their juices, the tomato purée and the white wine and simmer, stirring often, for 30 minutes to reduce the wine slightly.

6 Add the snapper stock to the saucepan and cook over a gentle heat for 30 minutes. The soup should be bubbling lightly during this time.

7 Pass the soup through a conical sieve, pressing to extract all juices. Season the strained soup to taste with the salt and pepper and reheat to boiling point when ready to serve.

8 To cook the pasta, bring a large saucepan of water to a rolling boil, add the pasta and cook for 2 minutes. Strain and refresh the cooked pasta under cold water to stop the cooking process, then drain and toss in a little olive oil to prevent it sticking.

9 To serve, cut the snapper into 6 × 50 g pieces. Lightly oil the fillets with olive oil and grill until translucent.

10 Ladle the boiling soup into 6 deep bowls and add the tomato dice, hot pasta and grilled fish. Sprinkle with the shredded parsley and top with a generous dollop of aïoli. Serve immediately.

Serves 6

parmesan-crumbed

sardine fillets with crisp black noodle pancake, roasted tomato sauce and aïoli

The textures and flavours that make up this dish capture the spirit of balmy nights by the sea. Black noodles are a personal favourite and they complement the oily iodine taste of sardines, octopus and scallops in particular. Squid ink, available from fishmongers and some specialty food shops, gives the noodles their colour.

150 g fine breadcrumbs (made from day-old, crusty bread), sieved
100 g freshly grated parmesan cheese
½ teaspoon sea salt
½ teaspoon black peppercorns, freshly ground
½ teaspoon chilli powder
24 sardine fillets
rice flour
3 eggs, beaten
120 g brioche crumbs
3 tablespoons flat parsley leaves, finely sliced
30 ml olive oil
vegetable oil for deep-frying
6 teaspoons Aïoli (see page 76)

Black Ink Noodles
3 large (61 g) eggs
2 teaspoons olive oil
2 teaspoons squid or cuttlefish ink
320 g plain flour
pinch of sea salt
rice flour

Roasted Tomato Sauce
1 head of garlic
12 ripe tomatoes
75 ml olive oil
½ teaspoon sea salt
½ teaspoon black peppercorns, freshly ground

1 To make the Black Ink Noodles, blend the eggs, oil and squid ink in a food processor until well incorporated. Add the flour and salt and blend again until the dough forms a ball. Refrigerate the dough, wrapped in plastic food wrap, for 1 hour.

2 Divide the chilled dough into 6 pieces. Flatten each piece with a rolling pin and then work the dough through the rollers of a pasta machine, starting on the widest setting and working and stretching the dough each time until you reach the second-finest setting. Each time the dough passes through the rollers, sprinkle it with some rice flour to prevent it sticking. Pass each sheet of dough through the spaghetti cutters on the pasta machine. Hang the noodles over a broom handle until ready to cook.

3 Bring a large saucepan of water to a rapid boil and cook the noodles for 2 minutes. Refresh the noodles immediately under cold, running water to stop the cooking. Drain, toss in a little oil and set aside.

4 To make the Roasted Tomato Sauce, preheat the oven to 300°C or as high as it will go. Brush a baking tray with a little olive oil and wrap the head of garlic in foil. Bake the garlic and tomatoes for 30 minutes until the tomatoes have coloured and the skins have split and the garlic has softened (the cloves should fall out of their skins when squeezed).

5 Pass the roasted tomatoes and garlic through a conical sieve, pressing firmly to extract all juices. While the mixture is still hot, blend in a food processor, adding the oil in a slow drizzle to bind the sauce. Season with salt and pepper.

6 To prepare the sardines, mix the breadcrumbs, half the parmesan cheese, salt, pepper and chilli powder in a bowl.

7 Dust the sardine fillets with rice flour, then coat with egg and then with the breadcrumb mixture. Arrange the sardines on a tray in a single layer and refrigerate until ready to cook.

8 To make the noodle pancakes, mix together the cooked noodles, brioche crumbs, remaining parmesan, parsley and olive oil. Heat a 12 cm cast-iron frying pan and brush it with oil. Distribute some crumbed noodles evenly over the base of the pan and cook over a medium heat until the noodles start to crisp. Flip over the noodle pancake and cook the other side. Turn out onto a warm plate and repeat the process until you have the necessary number of serves.

9 Heat the prepared tomato sauce until it comes to a boil.

10 Heat vegetable oil in a deep-fryer or saucepan until it reaches 180°C and fry the sardine fillets 6 at a time until they puff up in the oil (this usually takes only 2 minutes). Cook the sardines in small batches so the oil temperature doesn't drop, making the fish oil-sodden.

11 Spoon the hot sauce onto the plates, top with a crisp noodle pancake and layer the sardine fillets on top. Finish with a dollop of Aïoli.

Serves 6

Parmesan-crumbed Sardine Fillets with Crisp Black Noodle Pancake, Roasted Tomato Sauce and Aïoli

squid stuffed with bacon, capsicum and herbs with salsa verde and rouille

When preparing this dish, you need to obtain squid tubes of even size for a common cooking time. The squid can be stuffed and prepared up to a day in advance, so you don't need to get yourself into a mad panic at the last minute. Follow the principle of organising yourself beforehand and you can produce a miraculous feast with ease. These flavours and textures make the palate feel alive – there is depth, complexity and strength. The Salsa Verde used here, a heavenly paste from Italy's Emilian region, is a must to have on hand. Its uses are diverse and it provides an instant addition to an antipasto plate, livens up a piece of grilled or barbecued meat or fish and can even be spread on crusty bread to appease a hunger attack. It's quick and simple to make and is best eaten within a week of being made.

6 squid (each 12 cm long)
1 tablespoon diced onion
3 cloves garlic, minced
1 red bird's-eye chilli, minced
100 ml olive oil
160 g rindless bacon slices, cut into matchstick lengths
40 g fresh breadcrumbs (made from crusty white bread)
20 g roasted red capsicum, diced
20 g roasted yellow capsicum, diced
2 teaspoons shredded parsley leaves
2 teaspoons shredded basil leaves
1 teaspoon thyme leaves
25 g salted, tiny capers, rinsed thoroughly
3 anchovy fillets, chopped
50 ml lemon juice, strained
½ teaspoon sea salt
½ teaspoon black peppercorns, freshly ground
2 litres fish stock
6 teaspoons Rouille (see page 78)

Salsa Verde
25 g stale white bread
100 ml olive oil
75 g flat parsley leaves
40 g small capers, rinsed
2 large cloves garlic, minced
3 anchovy fillets, chopped
1 tablespoon finely minced red onion
30 ml lemon juice, strained
½ teaspoon black peppercorns, freshly ground

1 Clean each squid by removing the tentacles and internal sac. Discard the sac and lightly oil the tentacles and set aside. Remove the transparent pen from the body section and discard. Cut the wings away from the body, mince finely and set aside. Ensure the squid tubes are clean and free of membrane and rinse well under cold, running water.

2 Sauté the onion, garlic and chilli in the olive oil in a frying pan until the onion is golden and soft. Transfer the mixture to a bowl.

3 Fry the bacon in another pan to render it of its fat until it is slightly crisp. Drain and add to the onion mixture with the breadcrumbs, capsicums, herbs, capers, anchovy and minced squid wings. (If the mixture feels a little dry at this stage, add some more oil, but only enough to wet the mixture.) Season with lemon juice, salt and pepper.

4 Spoon the stuffing into the squid tubes until nearly full. Pack it tightly to ensure there are no air pockets and sew across the tops with a needle and thread to secure.

5 To make the Salsa Verde, soak the bread in a tablespoon of the oil. In a food processor, blend the parsley, capers, garlic, anchovy, onion, lemon juice and soaked bread until smooth. With the motor still running, slowly drizzle in the remaining olive oil until the mixture has emulsified. Season with pepper, taste and adjust if necessary. To store, spoon into a jar, seal and refrigerate.

6 Heat the fish stock in a wide-based braising pan until it comes to a boil. Turn to low and add the squid tubes. Cook them very gently in the stock for 20 minutes or until they feel firm to the touch. Roll regularly with a slotted spoon to ensure even cooking. They should float in a single layer in the pan, not on top of each other. Remove the cooked squid tubes carefully from the stock and allow to rest for a few minutes before slicing (letting the stuffing settle prevents them from splattering).

7 Just before serving, heat a frying pan and quickly toss the reserved squid tentacles over high heat for a minute or two only until they just start to curl. Season lightly.

8 To serve, spread the Salsa Verde on 6 plates, slice the squid into thin diagonal rounds and arrange on the sauce. Top with the fried squid tentacles and a dollop of Rouille. Serve immediately.

Serves 6

grilled rare tuna steak with fennel, green garlic and roasted garlic aïoli

This is a wonderful, easy-to-prepare number for a summer lunch or outdoor dinner that blends the subtle flavour of green garlic (immature garlic picked before the cloves have developed) with the aniseed taste of fresh fennel in a gently stewed lemon emulsion that complements the oiliness of the tuna and aïoli. The best results are achieved by minimal cooking. Well-cooked tuna belongs in a can, so if you go to the bother of buying a beautiful piece of fresh tuna, do it justice and cook it rare.

6 × 150 g trimmed tuna steaks (2 cm thick)
100 ml olive oil
2 small bulbs fennel, finely sliced
3 green garlic stems, finely sliced
5 cocktail onions, caramelised and cut into quarters
25 ml lemon juice, strained
50 ml virgin olive oil
pinch of sea salt
pinch of freshly ground white pepper
3 teaspoons chopped green fennel tops
6 tablespoons Roasted Garlic Aïoli (see page 77)

1 Preheat a chargrill pan or barbecue. Brush the tuna steaks with half the olive oil and set aside.

2 Heat a frying pan, add the remaining olive oil and gently sauté the fennel and green garlic until just softened. Add the caramelised onion and warm through. Transfer the vegetables to a bowl.

3 Make a vinaigrette by mixing the lemon juice and virgin olive oil with the salt and pepper. Stir the vinaigrette into the fennel mixture with the fennel tops, then spoon the vegetables onto 6 serving plates.

4 Quickly sear the tuna steaks on the hot grill for 1 minute on each side – just enough to seal and colour the surface, leaving the inside very rare and pink but warmed through.

5 Put the fish on the sautéd fennel and garlic and spoon over some aïoli. Serve immediately.

Serves 6

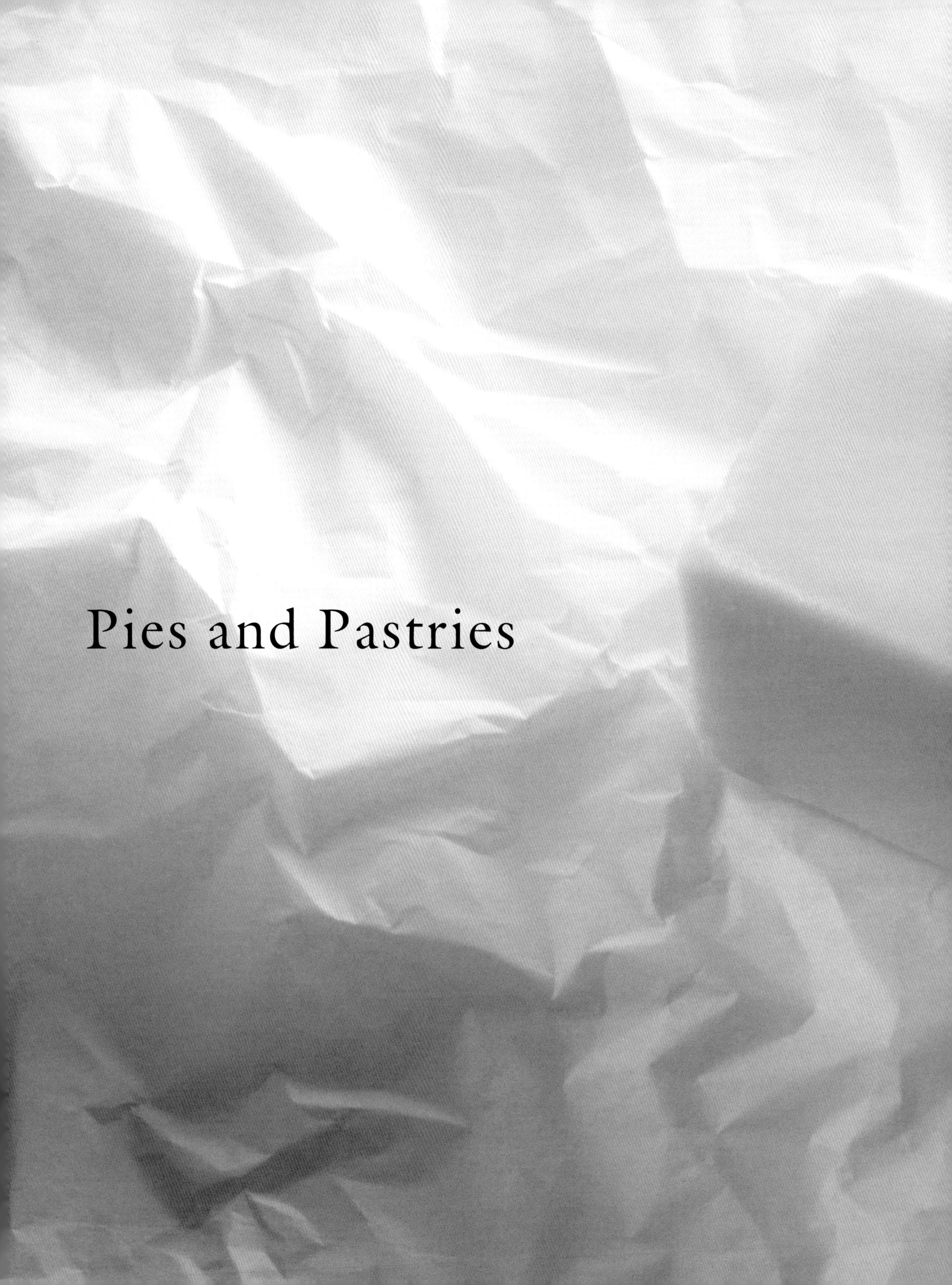

Pies and Pastries

In professional haute-cuisine cooking, pastry is traditionally studied and practised separately from the rest of the cooking process, such is its depth and intensity. I find it an interesting, challenging and productive part of my cooking repertoire. The uses for pastry are many and varied; it is the perfect receptacle for carrying other foods.

Making pastry requires patience, care, feeling and skill. It can be fickle and bothersome, difficult and contrary until you develop a deft hand, feel and understanding for it. It requires only a few basic concepts to understand and achieve the most rewarding results. As with any other aspect of cooking, there are certain rules to follow and procedures to adopt to guarantee a successful result. Temperature (of the ingredients, room, equipment and workbench) is one of the primary deciding factors. Pastry must be made and dealt with in a cool environment (under 18°C) with the fat content (butter, shortening, cream and so on) best at refrigerator temperature. Proceed with pastry preparation for short intervals to ensure that the correct temperature is maintained and not varied. It is also important not to overwork the dough; the gluten should remain undeveloped, unlike bread where the opposite rule of thumb applies.

The way the fat, flour, liquid and sugar react together depends on the way the pastry is constructed: elasticity is created through beating, as in a brioche; incorporating butter through repeated rolling and folding produces puff pastry, and working the pastry dough quickly to inhibit gluten development results in short, sweet and shortbread pastry doughs. As with most things in cooking, the quality of the ingredients and careful handling bear a direct relationship to the final outcome. Resting pastry in the refrigerator between the making, the rolling and the baking is of paramount importance, as it prevents shrinkage and allows the glutens to relax.

When making most of the pastry doughs in this chapter, any excess quantity can be wrapped and frozen for later use. Prepared pastry kept frozen can often come in handy at the last minute.

shortcrust pastry

This is the most simple and straightforward of all the pastry doughs and is very versatile. It is a more resistant pastry to use for tarts as it has the capacity to hold juicy and wet fillings without leaking or becoming soggy. This pastry will yield 12 individual tart cases or 2 × 20 cm tart cases and can be made in advance and frozen.

240 g plain flour
½ teaspoon sea salt
180 g unsalted butter, chilled and diced
80 ml sparkling mineral water, chilled

1 Chill the bowl and blade of a food processor in the refrigerator.

2 Blend the flour, salt and butter in the cold food processor bowl until the mixture resembles breadcrumbs.

3 Pour in the mineral water with the motor running and blend until the dough forms a ball. Wrap the dough in plastic foodwrap and rest for 1 hour in the refrigerator.

4 Roll out and cut the pastry according to the directions of the recipe and refrigerate for 30 minutes before baking.

sweet pastry

When sugar is added to pastry, it produces a crisper pastry that is similar to short-crust. This is quite a resistant and versatile pastry to use when making desserts or sweet things. As with the other pastries, work quickly to stop the glutens from developing, ensure all ingredients are of the same temperature to prevent shrinkage and rest the pastry in the refrigerator between making, rolling and baking. I usually bake it blind before filling it. This pastry will yield 6 individual tart cases or 1 × 20 cm tart case and can be made in advance and frozen.

50 g icing sugar
125 g plain flour
75 g unsalted butter, chilled and diced
2 egg yolks
seeds from ½ vanilla pod

1 Chill the bowl and blade of a food processor in the refrigerator.

2 Sift the icing sugar and the flour and incorporate with the butter in the food processor until the mixture resembles fine breadcrumbs.

3 Add the yolks and vanilla seeds and blend until the dough just comes together. Wrap the dough in plastic foodwrap and rest in the refrigerator for 2 hours.

4 Roll out and cut the pastry according to the directions of the recipe and refrigerate for 30 minutes before baking.

shortbread pastry

A higher ratio of fat to flour produces a shorter pastry that is harder to handle and softer in texture than others with more flour. This pastry is fragile and is at its best when served fresh as it is highly perishable. It can be used as a base for a tart or rolled and cut out to make biscuits. This quantity will yield 20 × 6 cm biscuits or a 20 cm tart shell. If used to line a tart tin, prick the base with a fork before resting so the pastry holds its shape during cooking. This pastry can be made in advance and frozen.

100 g unsalted butter
50 g icing sugar
1 egg yolk
1/2 tsp vanilla essence
125 g plain flour

1 Chill the bowl and blade of a food processor in the refrigerator.

2 Cream the butter in the food processor until soft. Sift in the icing sugar and work until thoroughly blended. Add the egg yolk and vanilla and mix lightly. Sift in the flour and pulse until the dough just comes together. Wrap the dough in plastic foodwrap and rest in the refrigerator for at least 2 hours.

3 Roll out and cut the pastry according to the directions of the recipe and refrigerate for 1 hour before baking.

chocolate pastry

This is a fabulous pastry from one of Australia's most celebrated chefs and culinary writers, Stephanie Alexander. It is like a chocolate shortbread, very moist with a fine crumb and used as a base for Chocolate Mocha Tart (see page 131). It can also be used to hold other chocolate fillings, such as chocolate mousse or chocolate butter cream.
Unlike other pastries, I find it easier to work this pastry into the tart shell as soon as it has been made, while it is still soft and pliable, using my fingers to press it into the shape of the tin. I have never had much success at rolling it out after it has become firm in the refrigerator. This quantity will yield 1 × 24 cm tart shell.

85 g unsalted butter, softened
85 g castor sugar
1/2 teaspoon vanilla essence
100 g plain flour
35 g Dutch cocoa

1 Cream the softened butter and the sugar together in an electric mixer (or by hand) until pale. Mix in the vanilla.

2 Sift the flour and cocoa together and mix into the butter until a dough is formed. The dough will feel quite wet.

3 Grease a 24 cm fluted flan tin, preferably one with a removable base, and press the pastry into the sides and over the base with your fingertips, ensuring it is evenly distributed. Allow the pastry shell to rest in the refrigerator for 1 hour.

4 Bake the pastry shell for 10 minutes in a 180°C oven. The pastry will bubble up slightly and slip down the sides a little, so when you take it out of the oven, and while it is still hot and malleable, press the pastry back into its original shape using a clean tea towel. Work quickly because once the pastry cools it holds its shape.

puff pastry

The nature of puff pastry lies in its preparation, where the layers of butter and flour are multiplied through the process of repeated folding and rolling. With the application of heat, the air that has been trapped between the layers expands and the water evaporates, causing the layers to separate and push up. It is the most complicated pastry to make, temperature being as important as the resting time between turns; the surface of the dough must not be broken during the rolling process or the butter will escape. I find this quantity of pastry most satisfying to work with. Follow the instructions and cut out the pastry into desired weights and freeze them for further use. Once cooked, this pastry should be served the same day as it deflates when stored.

500 g plain flour
250 ml sparkling mineral water, chilled
1 teaspoon sea salt
1/2 teaspoon strained lemon juice
250 g unsalted butter, chilled

1 Chill the bowl and blade of a food processor in the refrigerator.

2 Process the flour, salt, lemon juice and mineral water in the food processor bowl until incorporated. Refrigerate for 1 hour.

3 Rework the cold dough in the food processor a second time to work the glutens; this gives elasticity and prevents shrinkage. Wrap the dough in plastic foodwrap, making sure it is airtight. Rest for 1 hour in the refrigerator.

4 Roll the dough out on a cold surface to make a 40 cm × 30 cm rectangle about 1 cm thick.

5 Cut the cold butter into 1 cm thick slices and arrange in a single layer down the middle of the rectangle. Fold the edges in; the butter should be encased by the dough. It is important that the dough and the butter are of the same temperature and equal thickness to give uniformity to the layers when rolling. Flatten the dough with a rolling pin, dust with flour and refrigerate for 30 minutes, wrapped in plastic foodwrap.

6 Each time you work the pastry, dust it with flour and work on a cool surface. Using even pressure, roll the dough into a rectangle until it is 90 cm × 40 cm. Fold it over 3 times to end up with a piece of dough that is 30 cm × 40 cm. Turn the dough to your right and repeat the rolling and folding process, continuing until you have turned the dough twice.

7 Rest the dough in the refrigerator for 1 hour. (It is important to rest the dough at these intervals to prevent the dough from heating and to inhibit the glutens from building up through overworking.)

8 Continue the rolling and turning process until you have made 6 turns, refrigerating the dough for 1 hour after every second turn.

9 Roll and cut the pastry according to the directions of the recipe, brush with egg wash and refrigerate for 30 minutes before baking.

crème fraîche flaky pastry

This is a very short pastry because of the high ratio of fat to flour, which gives it its flakiness and richness. This pastry is best used for pies that have relatively dry fillings, as it does not need any extra moisture. It is not recommended for tart cases as it is too short and will crumble and fall apart. The pastry responds best when fresh and I don't recommend freezing it. This quantity will yield 6 individual pies or 1 large one.

190 g unsalted butter, chilled
300 g plain flour
½ teaspoon sea salt
190 g crème fraîche, chilled

1 Chill the bowl and blade of a food processor in the refrigerator.

2 Chop the butter into chunks and, while still cold, mix with the flour and salt in the cold food processor until the mixture resembles breadcrumbs.

3 Add the crème fraîche and pulse until the cream has just been incorporated. Don't overwork at this stage or the pastry will be quite difficult to handle when rolling.

4 Work the pastry into a ball by hand, wrap in plastic foodwrap and refrigerate for 2 hours.

5 Roll out and cut the pastry according to the directions of the recipe, brush with egg wash and refrigerate for 1 hour before baking.

sweet potato pastry

Chinese pastries are celebrated with the daily consumption of yum cha – a ritual of eating small amounts of many things, many encased in pastry. Chinese pastry differs from French pastry in its ingredients, construction and cooking. Dim-sum pastries are many and varied. There are pastry wrappers that are paper-thin and made from rice flour and water or with egg; spring-roll wrappers made with wheat flour; and dumpling pastries that use some form of vegetable starch as a base and are bound with duck fat, lard or oil. For this particular pastry I use sweet potato but it works with any other starchy root vegetable, such as potato, taro or yam. The dough is quite moist and needs to be worked on a bench floured with tapioca starch to stop it from getting sticky. When the pastries are filled and deep-fried, they become very puffy, flaky and aerated, with the filling steamed inside. This quantity will yield 24 dumplings.

750 g sweet potato, peeled and cubed
25 g castor sugar
40 g tapioca flour
25 g sweet potato flour
pinch of five-spice powder
60 ml vegetable oil
extra vegetable oil for deep-frying

1 Steam the sweet potato until soft and mash it while hot.

2 Mix all the ingredients together in a food processor. Remove the dough, wrap it in plastic foodwrap and allow it to rest in the refrigerator for 1 hour until firm.

3 Knead the dough and shape into the size of golf balls. Dust your hands with tapioca flour and flatten each ball into a flat disc about 4 cm in diameter. Put a teaspoon of your chosen filling onto the centre of each disc.

4 Fold each pastry over into a half-moon shape and press the edges together (you may need to use a little water to seal the edges). Rest the pastries on a floured tray until ready to cook.

5 Deep-fry 6 pastries at a time until golden and flaky and they float on the surface of the oil. This will take about 4 minutes. Drain on paper towels and serve hot.

Serves 8

brioche dough

Brioche is a type of bread dough, leavened with yeast and made rich with the addition of eggs and butter. The dough is beaten with a dough hook until it becomes very elastic and shiny and can be used to encase savoury or sweet fillings. Because of its elasticity, this pastry can withstand fillings that are quite wet but not too sloppy. The quantity given here will yield one brioche loaf baked in a regular-sized bread tin (ideal for breakfast) or will be enough to make any of the brioche recipes that follow.

250 g plain flour
pinch of sea salt
10 g compressed fresh yeast
50 ml warm milk
1 tablespoon castor sugar
2 large (61 g) eggs
125 g unsalted butter, softened

1 Put the flour and salt in the bowl of an electric mixer. In another bowl, mix the yeast into the warm milk with the sugar.

2 Whisk the eggs. Incorporate the yeast mixture into the flour with a dough hook on low speed. Add the eggs and turn the speed up to high. Mix for 5 minutes or until the dough appears elastic. Add the butter in small chunks until combined and the dough is smooth and shiny.

3 Put the dough into a greased bowl, cover with plastic foodwrap and allow to rise in a warm place for about 45 minutes or until it has doubled in size.

4 Punch the dough down and roll or knead it. Proceed according to the directions of the recipe. If making a loaf, put the dough into a bread tin, brush the surface with egg wash and allow the brioche to rise in a draught-free, warm place for 30 minutes. Bake the loaf over a water bath at 200°C for 40 minutes or until a skewer comes out clean. Turn onto a wire rack to cool.

baked goat's cheese tart with rocket and pickled walnut salad

Another perennial favourite on the Restaurant menu, this tart is made and baked to order and the balance between the cheese, custard, rocket and walnuts is perfect. You can make these tarts as individual ones, as a larger one or even as tiny tartlets that can be served as a canapé or appetiser (remember that the cooking time will vary accordingly). This tart was devised as a tribute to the wonderful fresh goat's cheeses being made in Australia, particularly by Gabrielle Kervella at Gidgegannup, Western Australia, and David Brown at Milawa, Victoria.

1 quantity of Shortcrust Pastry (see page 88)
6 large (61 g) eggs
3 teaspoons crème fraîche
1/4 teaspoon sea salt
1/4 teaspoon white peppercorns, freshly ground
6 teaspoons caramelised onions
6 tablespoons crumbled fresh goat's cheese
2 handfuls of perfect rocket leaves, trimmed
6 teaspoons finely diced red onion
3 pickled walnuts, sliced
30 ml balsamic vinegar
30 ml walnut oil
75 ml virgin olive oil
pinch of sea salt
pinch of freshly ground black pepper

1 Roll the pastry out on a cool, floured surface and line 6 × 12 cm Teflon flan tins. Refrigerate the pastry shells for 30 minutes.

2 Preheat the oven to 180°C. Blind bake the pastry shells for 20 minutes. Remove the paper and rice weights and let the tart shells cool. Leave the oven on.

3 Make a custard by whisking together the eggs, crème fraîche, salt and pepper.

4 Spoon the caramelised onion over the bases of the tart shells, add the crumbled goat's cheese and pour the custard over gently until the tart shells are full. Bake for 9 minutes until the custard has just set. The tart filling should have the same consistency as a soufflé mix, not too firm or the eggs will be overcooked and dry.

5 Carefully lift the baked tarts out of their tins onto plates and serve with a salad made at the last minute with the rocket leaves, red onion dice and pickled walnuts, dressed with a vinaigrette made with the vinegar, oils and the salt and pepper.

Serves 6

deep-fried sweet potato dumplings filled with prawn, chicken and water chestnuts

We serve these pastries at the Restaurant as an entrée with a chilli sauce or float one in a sweet potato soup. Either way, they are delectable. They will keep, refrigerated, up to 24 hours before they need to be cooked.

500 ml chicken stock
2 chicken breasts
25 ml fish sauce
15 ml fresh lime juice, strained
40 ml tamarind juice
2 tablespoons mint leaves
1 teaspoon jasmine rice, roasted and ground
200 g green prawn meat
1 tablespoon water chestnuts, blanched and finely chopped
1 tablespoon straw mushrooms, blanched and finely chopped
1 quantity of Sweet Potato Pastry (see page 94)

Coriander Paste
2 teaspoons minced garlic
1/2 teaspoon black peppercorns, freshly ground
a few sichuan peppercorns, ground
3 coriander roots
25 ml vegetable oil
2 teaspoons fish sauce
2 teaspoons strained lime juice
1/2 cup coriander leaves, chopped

1 To make the Coriander Paste, fry the garlic, peppers and coriander roots in the oil until softened and fragrant. Remove from the heat and stir in the fish sauce, lime juice and coriander leaves. Refrigerate until ready to use.

2 Bring the chicken stock to a boil in a saucepan and reduce the heat. Simmer the chicken breasts for 8 minutes. Turn off the heat and allow the meat to sit in the stock for another 5 minutes.

3 Remove the breasts from the stock, chop up roughly and blend in a food processor with the fish sauce, lime juice, tamarind juice, mint and ground rice until the mixture resembles mince. Do not overwork – the meat should not become a paste. Allow the mince to cool.

4 In a large bowl, mix together the chicken mince, prawn meat, water chestnuts, straw mushrooms and 1 tablespoon of the Coriander Paste.

5 Assemble and cook the dumplings according to the directions in the recipe for the Sweet Potato Pastry (see page 94).

Makes 18

five-spice duck and shiitake mushroom pies with ginger glaze

This pie made its début on our menu at the Phoenix and has been a permanent fixture since. The outward appearance of the pie pays homage to the French pithivier, *a hand-moulded dome, while its filling looks towards China. This dish is proof that the humble pie can achieve elegant status and refined technique. Start the preparations at least a day in advance. The duck can be cooked and the sauce and pastry made ahead of time, leaving only the assembly.*

1 × 1.7 kg duck, cleaned and trimmed
1 large brown onion, diced
3 cloves garlic, chopped
1 teaspoon chopped ginger
1 red chilli, split open
2 spring onions, chopped
100 ml vegetable oil
1 whole star anise
1 teaspoon fennel seeds
1 teaspoon sichuan peppercorns
2 litres duck stock
1 quantity of Crème Fraîche Flaky Pastry (see page 93)
egg wash

Ginger Glaze
60 ml vegetable oil
20 ml sesame oil
1 brown onion, chopped
3 cloves garlic, chopped
1 tablespoon finely shredded ginger
1 red bird's-eye chilli, split open
2 spring onions, chopped
1 whole star anise
1 teaspoon fennel seeds
1 teaspoon sichuan peppercorns
1 piece cassia bark
100 ml Stone's Green Ginger Wine
30 ml Chinese brown rice wine (shaosing)
20 ml fresh ginger juice
extra 1 tablespoon finely shredded ginger

Shiitake Mushroom Mix
50 g dried Chinese black mushrooms
1 brown onion, finely diced
2 cloves garlic, minced
2 teaspoons minced ginger
50 ml vegetable oil
200 g shiitake mushrooms, finely sliced
3 spring onions, finely sliced
2 teaspoons five-spice powder
1 teaspoon sea salt
1 teaspoon freshly ground black pepper
2 teaspoons flat parsley leaves, finely sliced

1 Begin preparing the duck at least a day before. Prick the duck all over with a skewer to release the fat and fry in vegetable oil until the skin is golden. Set aside.

2 In a deep-sided saucepan just big enough to hold the duck, fry the onion, garlic, ginger, chilli and spring onion until fragrant. Add the star anise, fennel seeds and sichuan peppercorns and stir until fragrant. Add the stock and bring to a boil. Reduce the heat, add the whole duck and simmer until the meat feels tender and is almost falling off the bone (this will take about 1½ hours). Turn the duck over a couple of times to ensure even cooking.

3 Remove the duck from the stock and allow to cool enough to handle. Strain the stock and skim off any fat. Refrigerate overnight for later use in the Ginger Glaze.

4 While the duck is still warm, take off all the meat, discarding the rest. Shred into uniformly small pieces and set aside.

5 The next day, make the Ginger Glaze (this will take about 2 hours). Heat a large saucepan and add the oils. Fry the onion, garlic, ginger, chilli and spring onion until softened. Stir in the star anise, fennel seeds, sichuan peppercorns and cassia bark and cook until fragrant. Deglaze the saucepan with the wines and cook, stirring, until reduced slightly.

6 Discard any fat from the reserved duck stock. Add the ginger juice and the duck stock and bring to a boil. Reduce the heat so the stock continues at a gentle boil and cook, skimming occasionally, until the sauce is reduced by half and has developed a shiny and sticky glaze. Remove from the heat and pass through a sieve to remove any sediment. Allow the sauce to become cold and settled and skim off any fat.

7 To make the Shiitake Mushroom Mix, soak the dried mushrooms in hot water until softened, then slice finely. Cook the onion, garlic and ginger in the oil in a frying pan until fragrant and softened. Stir in the sliced shiitake and black mushrooms and cook for 15 minutes until soft and any liquid has evaporated. Add the spring onion and cook until just softened, then add the five-spice powder, salt, pepper and parsley. Set aside to cool.

8 Mix the duck meat with an equal amount of the mushroom mixture until well incorporated. Form the mixture into balls slightly larger than a tennis ball.

9 Roll out the pastry on a floured surface to 5 mm thickness. Cut 6 bases 14 cm in diameter and 6 lids 16 cm in diameter. Brush the bases with egg wash, sit the balls of filling on top and cover with the pastry. Press the edges together with your fingers and smooth with a paring knife. Brush the lids with egg wash and score 6 or 7 arcs around the dome, working from the top centre down. Refrigerate the pies for at least 1 hour before baking.

10 Preheat the oven to 220°C. Bake the pies for 16 minutes on a baking tray until golden.

11 To reheat the Ginger Glaze, bring to a boil and add the extra ginger at the last minute. Use a spatula to slide the cooked pies from the tray to each plate. Serve with the glaze.

Serves 6

puff pastry baked with meredith farm sheep milk blue cheese and apple jelly

This pastry provides an interesting alternative to the usual cheese plate. I sometimes include it on a set menu as a small taste between main course and dessert. It is also ideal as a follow-up to a light lunch. Other boutique cheeses being made in Australia that would be equally suitable include Milawa Chevre or Milawa Blue, or even Kervella's Affiné, a matured goat's milk cheese. Of course, French roquefort or Italian gorgonzola will work just as well, depending on your preference.

½ quantity of Puff Pastry (see page 92)
250 g Meredith Farm Sheep Milk Blue Cheese
egg wash
6 tablespoons Apple Jelly (see page 142)

1 Roll out the pastry on a cool, floured surface and cut 6 rectangles each measuring 8 cm square and 1 cm thickness.

2 Cut 6 slices of the cheese the same size as the pastry.

3 Put the pastry sheets on a baking tray, brush with egg wash and score the tops diagonally with a sharp knife. Refrigerate the pastry until very cold again before baking.

4 Preheat the oven to 200°C. Bake the pastry sheets for 8 minutes or until golden. Remove from the oven and allow to cool on a wire rack. Reduce the oven temperature to 150°C.

5 Split the pastries open through the centre, spread each side carefully with Apple Jelly, put a slice of the cheese on each pastry base and top with the pastry lid.

6 Bake for 4 minutes until the cheese starts to soften. Serve immediately.

Serves 6

ocean trout fillet, leeks and mushrooms baked in pastry with tomato chive sauce and salmon roe

This is an adaptation of coulibiac, *which is a hot fish pie of Russian origin made popular by the French. It is a wonderful pie to cook for a group of friends. The preparation is done beforehand, so you will not be slaving over the stove and missing all the fun; when the pie is ready, you simply slice and serve it. At the Restaurant, we make this as a smaller individual piece as, once it is cooked, it needs to be served and eaten immediately. It is equally delicious made with freshwater salmon.*
The Tomato Chive Sauce can be made ahead of time up to the stage where the butter is added. Once the butter has been added, the sauce must be served immediately. I suggest you use the time the fish is baking to finish off the sauce.

1 × 1 kg ocean trout fillet
50 g butter
6 leeks, washed and finely sliced
1 tablespoon chopped garlic chives
sea salt
freshly ground white pepper
6 shallots, finely sliced
24 swiss brown or button mushrooms, sliced
1 quantity of Crème Fraîche Flaky Pastry (see page 93)
egg wash
6 teaspoons fresh salmon roe

Tomato Chive Sauce
1 brown onion, sliced
175 g unsalted butter
100 ml riesling or other white wine
6 ripe tomatoes
75 ml thick (45%) cream
1 teaspoon sea salt
1 teaspoon white peppercorns, freshly ground
3 tablespoons finely chopped chives

1 To make the Tomato Chive Sauce, sweat the onion in 25 g of the butter in a saucepan until softened. Add the white wine, bring to a boil and reduce by a third.

2 Purée the tomatoes in a food processor, add to the saucepan and cook until the liquid has been reduced by half again.

3 Pass the sauce through a conical sieve, pressing firmly to extract as much juice and pulp as possible. Discard the remaining solids.

4 In a clean saucepan bring the tomato sauce base and the cream to a boil. Set aside.

5 Trim the fish, removing its skin and bones and cutting away the tail end and belly piece to leave a fillet of even thickness weighing about 750 g. The fillet must be a constant thickness to ensure even cooking in the pastry.

6 Melt half the butter in a frying pan and gently sauté the leek until softened. Stir in the chives, season with a little salt and pepper and cool.

7 Melt the remaining butter in another frying pan and cook the shallots and mushrooms together until softened. Season with salt and pepper and cool.

8 Roll the pastry out on a cool, floured surface to make a 40 cm × 25 cm rectangle of 5 mm thickness. Brush the edges of the dough with egg wash. Spoon the mushroom mixture down the middle of the pastry, then put the fish on top and sprinkle with a little salt and pepper. Distribute the leeks evenly over the fish. Fold in the ends, then roll up the pastry to make a secure parcel. Rest seam-side down on a buttered baking tray. Brush the surface with the egg wash and refrigerate for 30 minutes before baking.

9 Preheat the oven to 220°C and bake the pie for 20 minutes until the pastry is cooked and golden – the fish should be just cooked. Don't be tempted to leave the pie in the oven any longer than 20 minutes.

10 Finish off the Tomato Chive Sauce while the pie is baking. Reheat over a medium heat and add the remaining butter, a piece at a time, stirring to incorporate each piece before adding the next (this is known as mounting the sauce). Stir constantly to prevent the sauce from separating. When all the butter has been added, take the saucepan off the heat and stir in the salt, pepper and chives. Taste and adjust if necessary.

11 To serve, cut the pie into 6 and put on serving plates. Spoon the sauce around and dot with some salmon roe.

Serves 6

Ocean Trout Fillet, Leeks and Mushrooms Baked in Pastry with Tomato Chive Sauce and Salmon Roe

baked apple and muscatel brioche with mascarpone

This is a popular patisserie item at the Store, where it is made each day and sold by the slice. You can experiment with other fruits and sweet fillings that take your fancy, the method remains the same. You can also serve the brioche with clotted cream if you wish.

1 quantity of Toffee Apples (see page 133)
50 g dried muscatels
60 g brown sugar
1 teaspoon ground cinnamon
250 g crème fraîche
2 teaspoons cornflour
1 quantity of Brioche Dough (see page 95)
egg wash
6 tablespoons Vanilla Mascarpone (see page 121)

1 Prepare the apples as directed and allow to cool.

2 Add the muscatels, brown sugar, cinnamon, crème fraîche and cornflour to the apples and mix well.

3 Roll out the brioche dough on a cool, floured surface to make a 30 cm × 18 cm rectangle of 1 cm thickness. Transfer the dough to a baking tray and brush the edges of the dough with egg wash. Place the filling along one long side of the dough. Fold in the ends, then fold the pastry over the filling and tuck it under so the parcel rests on its seam. Brush the surface with egg wash and allow the brioche to prove in a warm, draught-free place for 30 minutes.

4 Preheat the oven to 180°C and bake the brioche for 20 minutes or until golden.

5 Remove the brioche from the oven (sprinkle with some cinnamon sugar, if you like) and allow to cool slightly before slicing. Serve with a generous spoonful of Vanilla Mascarpone.

Serves 6

lemon tart with lemon verbena ice-cream

The classic lemon tart is a part of every self-respecting cook's repertoire. This particular recipe is an adaptation of Marco Pierre White's wonderful lemon tart from his book White Heat. *It is one of those things that demands to be eaten immediately as it does not keep well at all. Although some people serve this type of tart with cream, I prefer to accentuate the flavour with Lemon Verbena Ice-cream (see page 124), which, to my palate, is a much better complement to the tart. (We should move beyond the idea that cream is served on the side of every dessert, regardless of its content, structure and taste.) Of course, the tart is also perfect served unadorned, its beauty being its simplicity.*

1 quantity of Sweet Pastry, made with 1 teaspoon minced lemon zest (see page 89)
1 egg white, beaten
6 large (61 g) eggs
110 g castor sugar
450 ml thick (45%) cream
225 ml lemon juice, strained
1 quantity of Lemon Verbena Ice-cream (see page 124)

1 Roll out the pastry on a cool, floured surface and line a 20 cm flan tin that has been buttered. Refrigerate for 1 hour.

2 Brush the pastry with the beaten egg white and refrigerate for another 15 minutes.

3 Preheat the oven to 180°C and blind bake the pastry shell until lightly coloured, about 18 minutes. Remove from the oven.

4 Beat the eggs and sugar until pale and foamy. Mix in the cream, then add the lemon juice at the last minute. Pour the lemon custard into the hot pastry shell and bake until just set, 25–30 minutes. Remove from the oven and allow to cool for 30 minutes before removing from the flan tin. Dust with icing sugar, slice and serve immediately with Lemon Verbena Ice-cream.

Breads

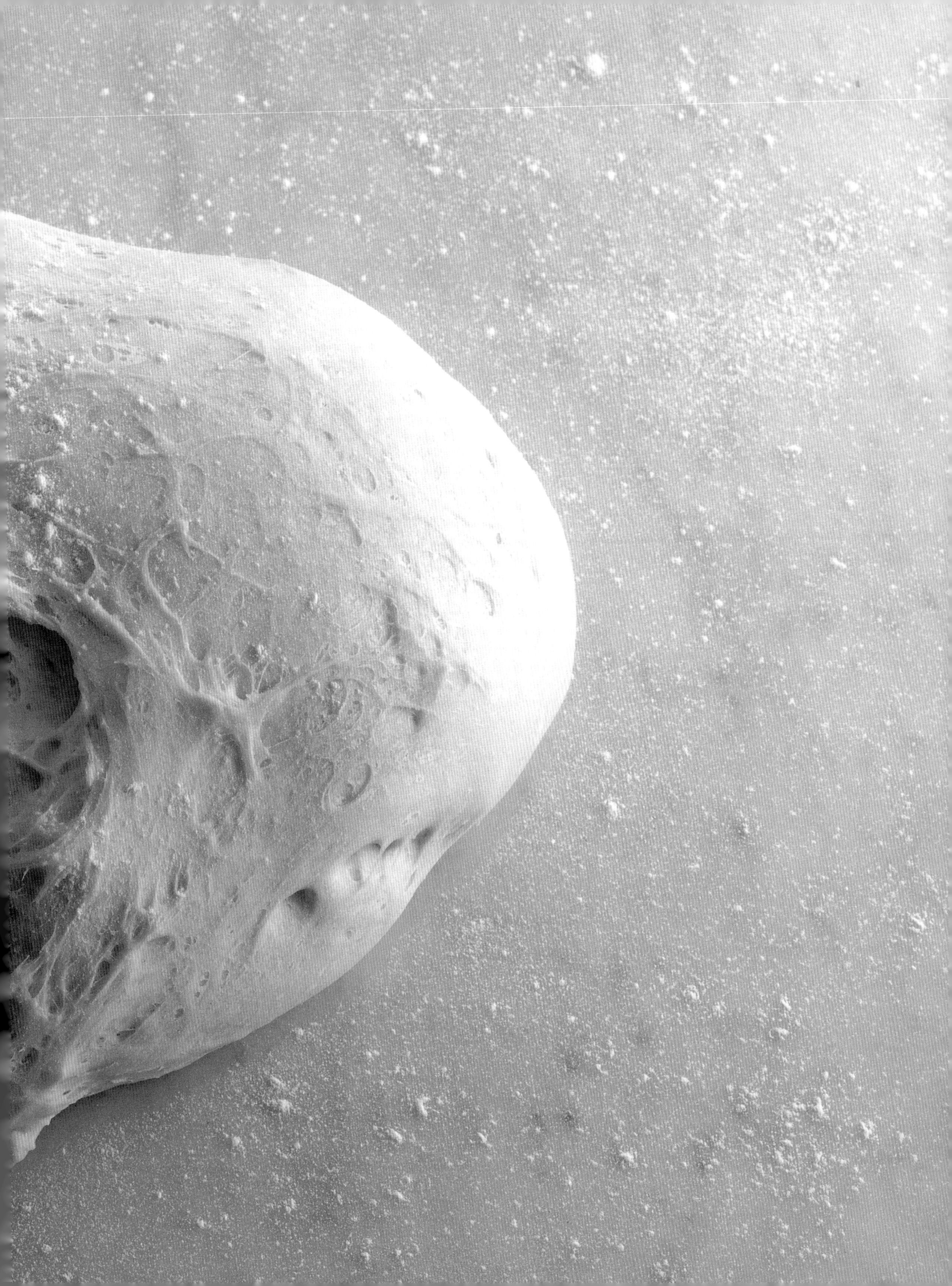

Bread is the staff of life, part of our historical development and a mainstay of our modern diet, offering roughage, energy, flavour and sustenance and acting as a carrier for other foods. The breaking of bread at the table symbolises a bond of friendship, giving and generosity. The making of bread is a comforting and empowering one, a response to some primal urge and a skill too often overlooked and ignored in our acceptance of the instant and the immediate. To understand and practise the art of breadmaking is to have a close relationship with a necessary food source and its preparation is an act of providing for our wellbeing!

I believe it is a moral sin to charge for bread when diners are paying for their food – it is mean-spirited. While there appears to be a resurgence of interest in good, well-made and tasty bread at the consumer level, this has not been translated into broad-based restaurant practice, with most establishments relying on a mass-produced, commercial and often inferior product. As a restaurateur, I adopt the philosophy that it is my responsibility to make and offer bread to customers as a sign of welcome. For me, a good cook means being generous, extravagant and knowledgeable and this should be apparent in all aspects of restaurant life. Anything else amounts to failure and a lack of soul.

The skill of breadmaking is easily acquired, especially through enthusiasm, practice and repetition. It requires a 'feel', particularly for texture and temperature, a good machine, strong arms and, most importantly, time. Strong flour is required to give the best results, that is, flour that has a higher gluten content than regular plain flour. Yeast has a life of its own and can be temperamental. When introduced to flour and water, it acts as a leavening agent, allowing the dough to rise and double in volume and become elastic. It can be obtained in fresh or dried form, depending on preference. The general rule is that a recipe calling for fresh yeast uses twice as much as dried yeast. Kneading is an important part of the process as it develops the glutens in the dough to give a lighter texture and finer crumb. Hand-kneaded bread usually has a denser texture and heavier feel than bread that has been worked by a machine.

For an even result and consistent crumb, allow the dough to double its volume in the first rising, then punch down the dough, knead and roll into the desired shape, glaze if necessary and allow the prepared dough to rise and double in volume a second time before baking. This second rising determines the look and feel of the bread. If fractures or cracks appear in the baking, it is usually because insufficient time was allowed for the second rising; the bread will feel heavier than it should and will have lost its shape. Remember that rising times are not absolute as how quickly the dough rises depends on the weather and the atmosphere in which you are working. Try to develop a feel for the dough so you can tell when it is ready, when it needs attention and so forth – instincts are much better than a clock! Failing the procedure a few times teaches you a lot more about the dynamics and what to look out for than an instant success.

The various ways we roll our bread are offered with each recipe but are not blueprints for reproduction; feel free to use your imagination. After all, texture and taste take precedence over shape, so this is where energies should be directed. Bread bakes best in a hot and humid oven, so it is advisable to spray the oven with water at regular intervals during baking to give a good crust. Baking bread on an unglazed clay tile in the bottom of the oven gives the bread a better crust again. Bread made with milk instead of water gives a softer dough with little or no crust.

At the Restaurant, we make bread for each service and three different kinds of bread are baked at the Store throughout the day. This chapter is an ode to the clever Barbara Alexander, the great cook who manages our Store and works closely with me in the Restaurant. She understands the importance of bread and how to make it and the good effect it can have. Her skill is matched by her imagination, and some of her creations are ingenious.

walnut bread

This is a very manageable bread dough to work with, easy to roll out, not at all sticky, and so a good starting point. It is a wonderful bread to serve with cheese, particularly the more pungent varieties. A generous slice of quince paste completes the equation.

500 g bread flour
1 teaspoon sea salt
200 g whole, shelled walnuts
20 g compressed fresh yeast
1 teaspoon castor sugar
250 ml warm water
2 tablespoons walnut oil
rice flour
1 egg yolk

1 Put the flour, salt and walnuts in the bowl of an electric mixer with a dough hook.

2 Dissolve the yeast and sugar in the warm water and then pour it into the flour with the walnut oil. Knead with the dough hook on medium speed for 15 minutes until the dough becomes quite elastic in appearance and spongy to feel. The dough should not feel sticky; if it does, then too much liquid has been used and the flour content will have to be adjusted.

3 Cover the bowl with plastic foodwrap and a tea towel and leave the dough to rise and double in volume in a warm, draught-free place for 1 hour.

4 When the dough has doubled in volume, remove it from the bowl onto a clean surface. Punch down the dough and knead by hand for a couple of minutes to continue working the glutens. Divide the mixture in 2 and roll each piece into a log about 50 cm long and 5 cm in diameter. Sprinkle over some rice flour and roll the logs in it to coat lightly. Tie each piece of dough into a loose knot. Sit the 2 bread knots on a baking tray and brush the tops with egg yolk.

5 Cover the loaves with a tea towel and allow to rise for 20 minutes until doubled in volume a second time.

6 Bake at 250°C for 15 minutes until the bread sounds hollow when tapped on its base and feels quite light. Cool on a wire rack.

Makes 2 loaves

olive breadsticks

These breadsticks are as easy to throw together as the walnut bread, the only preparation involved being the pitting of the olives. They are at their best served warm with soft, creamy cheese, sliced for picnic sandwiches, toasted and served with a selection of antipasti or served as a canapé topped with a piece of grilled fish and a dollop of tapenade.

500 g bread flour
1 teaspoon sea salt
200 g kalamata olives, pitted
20 g compressed fresh yeast
1 teaspoon castor sugar
250 ml warm water
rice flour
2 tablespoons olive oil
extra sea salt

1 Mix the flour, salt and olives together in the bowl of an electric mixer with a dough hook.

2 Dissolve the yeast and sugar in the warm water. Add the liquid to the flour and knead with the dough hook on medium speed for 15 minutes.

3 Cover the bowl with plastic foodwrap and a tea towel and leave the dough to rise and double in volume in a warm, draught-free place for 1 hour.

4 Take the dough out of the bowl, punch it down, knead on a clean surface and divide the mixture into 3 pieces. Roll each piece of dough into a long log shape and sprinkle lightly with rice flour. Put on a baking tray, leaving enough space for a second rising.

5 Cut a couple of diagonal slashes in the tops of the dough with a sharp knife or razor blade. Drizzle the olive oil over the slashes and glaze the top with it. Sprinkle with a little extra sea salt.

6 Cover the loaves with a tea towel and allow to rise for 20 minutes until doubled in volume a second time.

7 Bake at 250°C for 12 minutes or until the bread sounds hollow when tapped on its base and feels quite light. Cool on a wire rack.

Makes 2 loaves

corn bread

This bread has a denser texture than the other breads given here and keeps well for a few days. It lends itself well to being served with red meats and hearty winter stews, being toasted with cheddar cheese or grilled with bacon or pancetta or made into crisp croutons rubbed with garlic and thrown into a salad. Use only fine-ground polenta in the dough or the texture will be quite gritty.

500 g bread flour
250 g fine polenta
1 teaspoon sea salt
30 g compressed fresh yeast
1 teaspoon castor sugar
275 ml warm water
2 large eggs (61 g), at room temperature
1 egg yolk
a little extra polenta

1 Mix the flour, polenta and salt in the bowl of an electric mixer with a dough hook.

2 Dissolve the yeast and sugar in the warm water. Whisk the eggs and add to the yeast liquid. Add the liquid to the flour and knead with the dough hook on medium speed for 15 minutes.

3 Cover the bowl with plastic foodwrap and a tea towel and leave the dough to rise and double in volume in a warm, draught-free place for 1 hour.

4 Remove the dough from the bowl, punch it down and knead on a clean surface for a few minutes. Divide the dough in 2 and roll each piece into a ball. Rolling back and forth, and using the heels of the palms of your hands, push down on the edges of each ball of dough.

5 Glaze the top of each loaf with egg yolk and sprinkle lightly all over with the extra polenta. Slash the tops across diagonally once with a sharp knife or razor blade. Put the 2 loaves on a baking tray with enough room to allow for the second rising.

6 Cover the loaves with a tea towel and allow to rise for 20 minutes until doubled in volume a second time.

7 Bake at 250°C for 15 minutes until the bread sounds hollow when tapped on its base and feels quite light. Cool on a wire rack.

Makes 2 loaves

fruit and raisin bread

The fruit makes this quite a dense bread. Its character will be different from the other savoury breads given here, which are lighter in texture. It is delicious for breakfast toasted and served with your favourite jam, or sliced and served with Muscat-poached Fruit (see page 150) and clotted cream for dessert.

100 g dried figs, sliced
100 g dried apricots, sliced
100 g seedless raisins
500 g bread flour
1 teaspoon sea salt
1 teaspoon ground cinnamon
25 g compressed fresh yeast
100 g brown sugar
250 ml warm milk
1 large (61 g) egg, beaten
extra flour
1 egg yolk

1 Put the figs, apricots and raisins in a bowl and cover with boiling water. Allow to sit for 5 minutes until the fruit has been reconstituted. Strain the fruit and throw out the water.

2 Mix the flour, salt, cinnamon and fruit in the bowl of an electric mixer with a dough hook.

3 Dissolve the yeast and sugar in the warm milk and pour into the dry ingredients. Add the beaten egg and knead with the dough hook on medium speed for 20 minutes until the dough is well incorporated and elastic.

4 Cover the bowl with plastic foodwrap and a tea towel and leave the dough to rise and double in volume in a warm, draught-free place for 1 hour.

5 Punch down the dough, take it out of the bowl and knead for a couple of minutes on a clean surface. Divide the dough in 2 and roll each piece into an oblong loaf. Dust with extra flour, glaze with egg yolk and sit on a baking tray.

6 Cover the loaves with a tea towel and allow to rise for 20 minutes until doubled in volume a second time.

7 Bake at 250°C for 20 minutes until the bread sounds hollow when tapped on its base and feels quite light. Cool on a wire rack.

Makes 2 loaves

onion, nigella and yoghurt bread

This spicy bread is enhanced by the aromatic and fragrant flavours of rich curries, chilli-based food, tandoori and barbecued meats, pickles and spicy dips. The shape we make this particular bread in resembles Madonna's breast plates designed by Jean Paul Gaultier. It demands attention and asks to be eaten!

500 g bread flour
1 teaspoon sea salt
1 teaspoon nigella seeds
20 g compressed fresh yeast
1 teaspoon castor sugar
150 ml warm water
1 cup warmed caramelised onion
½ cup plain yoghurt, at room temperature
rice flour
1 egg yolk

1 Mix the flour, salt and nigella seeds in the bowl of an electric mixer with a dough hook.

2 Dissolve the yeast and sugar in the warm water, stir in the warm onion and the yoghurt and pour immediately into the flour. Knead with the dough hook on medium speed for 15 minutes.

3 Cover the bowl with plastic foodwrap and a tea towel and allow the dough to rise and double in volume in a warm, draught-free place for 1 hour.

4 Punch down the dough, turn out of the bowl onto a clean surface and knead for a few minutes until smooth and elastic. Divide the dough in 2 and roll each piece into a 60 cm long sausage and dust lightly with rice flour. Roll each length into a cone shape that stands about 12 cm high, starting from the base and working up. Stand the loaves on a baking tray and glaze with egg yolk.

5 Cover the loaves with a tea towel and allow to rise for 20 minutes until doubled in volume a second time.

6 Bake at 250°C for 15 minutes until the bread sounds hollow when tapped on its base and feels quite light. Cool on a wire rack.

Makes 2 loaves

Onion, Nigella and Yoghurt Bread

pumpkin and parmesan bread

The addition of roasted pumpkin makes this bread moist, flavoursome and very versatile. It is great served with pasta or soups or used as a base for sandwiches. It keeps quite well for a few days. Hang the expense and use the cheese suggested, don't on any account use the packet grated variety as the outcome will be nothing short of disappointing. Be economical elsewhere and let the flavour of the bread shine through.

1 small butternut pumpkin
500 g bread flour
50 g freshly grated reggiano parmesan cheese
1 teaspoon sea salt
1 teaspoon black peppercorns, freshly ground
25 g compressed fresh yeast
1 teaspoon castor sugar
125–150 ml warm water
rice flour
1 egg yolk
a little extra reggiano parmesan cheese

1 Bake the whole pumpkin at 180°C until soft. Scoop out 1½ cups flesh and mash. Allow the mashed pumpkin to cool to room temperature.

2 Mix together the flour, parmesan cheese, salt and pepper in the bowl of an electric mixer with a dough hook.

3 Dissolve the yeast and sugar in 125 ml of the warm water and add the 1½ cups mashed pumpkin. Pour this mixture into the dry ingredients and knead with the dough hook on medium speed for 20 minutes. Check the consistency of the dough; if it feels too dry, add a little extra warm water and continue kneading.

4 Cover the bowl with plastic foodwrap and a tea towel and leave the dough to rise and double in volume in a warm, draught-free place for 1 hour.

5 Punch down the dough, turn out onto a clean surface and knead for a couple of minutes. Divide the dough in 2 and roll each piece into a round loaf. Sprinkle each loaf with a little rice flour, glaze the tops with egg yolk and slash across the centre of each with a sharp knife or razor blade. Sprinkle with a little extra parmesan cheese and sit the loaves on a baking tray.

6 Cover the loaves with a tea towel and allow to rise for 20 minutes until doubled in volume a second time.

7 Bake at 250°C for 15 minutes until the bread sounds hollow when tapped on its base and feels quite light. Cool on a wire rack.

Makes 2 loaves

sun-dried tomato bread

This bread owes its tastiness to the tomato pesto that flavours it. The initial kneading needs to be watched to ensure the oil-based pesto works itself into the dough properly; the dough will feel slippery compared to other bread doughs. It is best to get used to the feel and baking of the other breads before plunging head first into this one. This bread is wonderful eaten straight from the oven, served with a roasted tomato or fish soup or used as a base for canapés or bruschetta and fabulous with a bowl of garlic prawns or fried sardines. This recipe can also be adapted to use Basil Pine Nut Pesto (see page 10) in place of the tomato pesto, the quantity and method being the same. Make sure the pestos are at room temperature.

If you are serious about the pursuit of breadmaking, may I suggest you read Bread *by James Beard,* English Bread and Yeast Cookery *by Elizabeth David,* The Italian Baker *by Carol Field and* Bread and Fermented Goods *by L. J. Hanneman.*

500 g bread flour
1 teaspoon sea salt
20 g compressed fresh yeast
1 teaspoon castor sugar
250 ml warm water
200 g Sun-dried Tomato Pesto (see page 12)
1 egg yolk

1 Mix the flour and salt in the bowl of an electric mixer with a dough hook.

2 Dissolve the yeast and sugar in the warm water, then stir in half the pesto. Pour into the dry ingredients and knead with the dough hook on medium speed for 10 minutes until the dough is well incorporated and elastic.

3 Cover the bowl with plastic foodwrap and a tea towel and allow to rise and double in volume in a warm, draught-free place for 1 hour.

4 Punch down the dough, turn out of the bowl onto a clean surface and knead for a few minutes until the dough comes back together (the oil will incorporate into the dough). Divide the dough in 2 and roll each piece into a rectangle 25 cm × 15 cm. Spread each piece of dough with the remaining pesto and, with the longest side facing you, roll up like a roulade. Put the rolls, seam-side down, on a baking tray and brush with egg yolk.

5 Cover the loaves with a tea towel and allow to rise for 20 minutes until doubled in volume a second time.

6 Bake at 250°C for 15 minutes until the bread sounds hollow when tapped on its base and feels quite light. Cool on a wire rack.

Makes 2 loaves

Sweet Curds and Creams

Dessert is an integral part of a meal, it provides balance and conclusion. It allows us to indulge in the sweet things of life, necessary luxuries that should be part of our daily ritual. Food is eaten for pleasure and purpose and it is within this context that I stress the important position of edible delights based on sugar and fat (the basic components of all desserts). There is no use in pretending they are not there by ignoring them, so liven up the tastebuds with a dash of sugar, served at the appropriate time, of course, and not to excess. Remember, too, that the cooking and proper execution of dessert is an exacting art, more so than other forms of cooking.

Nothing comes near well-made ice-cream and sorbets for that instant sweet hit of fruit and sugar, so refreshing in summer or even after a rich meal. Commercially made ice-creams, with their preservatives and chemicals, hold little appeal, their flavours often being lack-lustre. Ice-creams at the Paramount Restaurant are usually always moulded affairs; I learnt the skill of ice-cream construction from Phillip Searle. Moulded ice-creams date back to the time of Carême, a great French chef who, in the nineteenth century, considered 'the main branch of architecture [to be] confectionery'. He was the first chef to create extravagant edible constructions whose visual brilliance could be consumed. To read more about his work, refer to Anne Willan's *Great Cooks and their Recipes – from Taillevent to Escoffier*. In *Much Depends on Dinner*, Margaret Visser writes an eloquent chapter about the history of ice-cream, its phenomenon as a convenience food and its constant prestige and presence in a formal setting. For a greater insight and understanding of the making of ice-cream, you can do no better than to read Jane Grigson's *Good Things*, her evocative writing captures the imagination and gives you the courage to try.

Restaurant desserts should be spectacular; as it is often the last impression a diner leaves with, dessert should be memorable, making him or her long to return. At home, dessert need not be an elaborate affair but we should partake in the overwhelming abundance of fruit we have on hand. So, with the firm belief that desserts are delectable, desirable and a necessary sensual pleasure to be indulged in, I prepare them with the skill and adoration they deserve and trust they are consumed with equal passion.

thick vanilla cream

This very rich custard is similar in texture and consistency to brulée custard and lends itself very well as an accompaniment to many fruits. It is best used in individual tarts as it will not hold its shape when used to fill a large tart that has to be cut. It can be made a day or two ahead and kept refrigerated.

175 ml thick (45%) cream
½ vanilla pod, split open and scraped
3 large egg yolks
25 g castor sugar
¼ gelatine leaf

1 In a saucepan, heat the cream and vanilla seeds over a low heat to simmering point.

2 Whisk the egg yolks and sugar together in a bowl. Gently pour the hot cream into the egg and stir well. Cook the mixture over a bain-marie until the consistency of a thick custard (brulée).

3 Soak the gelatine leaf in cold water until softened, then squeeze out the water and stir into the custard until the gelatine has dissolved.

4 Whisk the custard over ice to cool. Refrigerate the cream until set.

passionfruit cream

Similar in preparation and texture to Thick Vanilla Cream, this intense-tasting cream is made sublime with the addition of fresh passionfruit juice. The taste makes the effort of getting the juice really worth your while! Make it when passionfruit are at their peak and in plentiful supply.

125 ml thick (45%) cream
3 large egg yolks
40 g castor sugar
60 ml passionfruit juice
½ gelatine leaf

1 Heat the cream to simmering point.

2 Whisk the egg yolks and sugar together in a bowl. Add the passionfruit juice and whisk again. Pour the warm cream over the egg mixture, stirring constantly.

3 Cook the cream mixture over a bain-marie until it reaches the consistency of thick custard, stirring constantly.

4 Soak the gelatine leaf in cold water until softened, then squeeze out the water and stir into the custard until the gelatine has dissolved.

5 Pass the cream through a fine-mesh sieve, cover with plastic film and refrigerate until cool and set.

chocolate cream

This is a simple ganache preparation that can be made ahead of time and reheated gently over a bain-marie. It can be used wherever a rich chocolate coating or layer is needed: to ice a cake, rolled into balls when firm and dusted with cocoa to serve with coffee or to sandwich meringues, fudge cake or shortbreads.

125 g dark couverture chocolate
100 ml thick (45%) cream

1 Shave the chocolate into a bowl.

2 Heat the cream to simmering point and pour over the chocolate. Stir until combined and glossy.

3 If using the cream as a filling, allow the cream to set in the refrigerator.

lemon curd

This is one of those delectable basics to always have on hand, even if you just want to spread it on toast. Use it to fill a 20 cm tart shell, spread it between layers of sponge or serve it in a pot alongside brioche toast and candied lemon. It is also referred to as lemon butter.

5 large egg yolks
100 g castor sugar
110 ml lemon juice, strained
125 g unsalted butter

1 Whisk the egg yolks and sugar until they are light and fluffy. Add the lemon juice and cook over a bain-marie until thick, stirring constantly.

2 Add the butter, piece by piece, allowing each piece to incorporate before adding the next. The mixture should have become thicker by the time the last piece of butter has been added. Remove from the heat and set the bowl over ice to cool.

3 To store, spoon into a jar and refrigerate.

vanilla mascarpone

Mascarpone is a cooked cream curd of northern Italian origin and has a texture similar to clotted cream but is not as high in fat. The method I use for making mascarpone has been adapted from that mentioned by Glynn Christian in his World Guide to Cheeses *but I add vanilla to give the mascarpone more depth of flavour. If you want to make a plain mascarpone, omit the vanilla. The mascarpone will keep, refrigerated, for 1 week.*

2 limes
1 litre single (35%) cream
1 vanilla pod, split open and scraped
1 scant teaspoon citric acid

1 Zest and juice the limes.

2 Bring the lime zest, cream and vanilla pod to a vigorous boil in a deep, stainless steel pot. Boil for 5 minutes until the cream separates.

3 Add the lime juice and citric acid to the cream and bring back to a boil. Simmer for 1 minute and remove from the heat. Pour the cream through a fine-mesh sieve into a bowl. Sit the bowl in the refrigerator until it starts to set.

4 Line a conical sieve with a double layer of wet muslin and sit it over a 2 litre bucket. Pour in the cream, cover the sieve with plastic and let the sieve stand for 24 hours to separate the whey from the curd.

5 Scoop the mascarpone into a plastic container, seal and refrigerate until ready to use.

passionfruit bavarois

A light, mousse-like cream tasting of passionfruit set just enough to still wobble, ethereal to the palate and one of my particular favourites. I am predictable in my constant use of passionfruit.

125 ml milk
4 large egg yolks
150 g castor sugar
100 ml passionfruit juice
2 gelatine leaves
250 ml thick (45%) cream, whipped until stiff

1 Heat the milk in a saucepan to simmering point.

2 Whisk the egg yolks and sugar together in a bowl until pale and creamy. Add the passionfruit juice, then whisk in the warm milk. Cook to the consistency of custard over a bain-marie, stirring constantly.

3 Soak the gelatine leaves in cold water until softened, then squeeze out the water and stir into the custard until the gelatine has dissolved.

4 Strain the custard through a fine-mesh sieve and cool over ice in the refrigerator. When almost set, whisk in the whipped cream.

5 Spoon the mixture into 6 plastic bavarois or dariole moulds and allow to set in the refrigerator for 4 hours or overnight, covered with plastic foodwrap.

6 To turn out each bavarois, hold the mould in hot water for a few seconds. Slide the custard out of its mould onto the serving plate.

Serves 6

honey bavarois

A bavarois is a flavoured custard base set lightly with gelatine and whipped cream and moulded before being turned out for serving. It gives the illusion of eating air, due to its ever-so-light texture, and takes on the intensity of the chosen flavouring. When making Honey Bavarois, choose a honey that has a flavour you like, but make sure it's not too strong or sweet otherwise it will mask the flavours of its accompaniment.

4 large egg yolks
100 g castor sugar
320 ml milk
60 ml honey
2½ gelatine leaves
250 ml thick (45%) cream

1 Whisk together the egg yolks and sugar in a bowl.

2 In a saucepan, heat the milk and honey to a simmer. Pour the milk onto the eggs, whisk and then stir over a bain-marie until the mixture is the consistency of custard.

3 Soak the gelatine leaves in cold water until soft, then squeeze out the water and stir into the custard until the gelatine has dissolved.

4 Strain the custard into a clean bowl and cool over ice.

5 Fold the cream into the cooled custard. Spoon the mixture into 6 plastic bavarois or dariole moulds and allow to set in the refrigerator for 4 hours or overnight, covered with plastic foodwrap.

6 To turn out each bavarois, hold the mould in hot water for a few seconds. Slide the custard out of its mould onto the serving plate.

Serves 6

pineapple sorbet with candied fruit

The best way to obtain fresh pineapple juice is to purée very ripe, sweet pineapples and pass the purée through a fine-mesh sieve. Alternatively, an electric juicer that produces fibre-free juices can be used.

75 g castor sugar
500 ml fresh pineapple juice, strained
1 tablespoon finely chopped glacé pineapple
1 tablespoon finely chopped candied citron (*cedru*)
100 g liquid glucose

1 Whisk the sugar into the pineapple juice with the glacé pineapple and the citron.

2 Melt the glucose in a bowl over a bain-marie until it becomes liquid and stir into the juice, mixing well.

3 Churn the mixture in an ice-cream machine according to the manufacturer's instructions. Store in the freezer.

raspberry sorbet

Sorbet has a more intense fruit flavour than ice-cream and when served with ice-cream it helps to cut some of the richness and creaminess – a great balance. Fresh raspberries need to be puréed and then passed through a fine-mesh sieve to give the required amount of juice. Raspberry seeds have no place in sorbet, the initial effort gives the most rewarding results.

125 g castor sugar
25 ml fresh lime juice, strained
750 ml sieved raspberry purée
150 g liquid glucose

1 Stir the sugar and lime juice into the raspberry purée until the sugar has dissolved.

2 Soften the glucose in a bowl over a bain-marie until it becomes liquid. Whisk the glucose into the purée until well incorporated.

3 Churn the mixture in an ice-cream machine according to the manufacturer's instructions. Store in the freezer.

Serves 6

lime mousse

This mousse is cooked slowly over a bain-marie like a custard, but is enriched with butter. The whipped cream is folded in when it has cooled to give it a mousse-like texture. The lime juice helps to counteract the fatty taste it would otherwise have.

5 large egg yolks
100 g castor sugar
1/4 teaspoon cornflour
110 ml fresh lime juice, strained
1 gelatine leaf
125 g unsalted butter
200 ml thick (45%) cream

1 Whisk the egg yolks and sugar in a bowl until light, then add the cornflour, followed by the lime juice. Place the bowl over a bain-marie and continue to whisk over heat until the mixture starts to thicken.

2 Soak the gelatine leaf in cold water until softened, then squeeze out the water and stir into the custard until the gelatine has dissolved.

3 Gradually add the butter to the custard a piece at a time, adding more as each piece melts into the custard, which should start to thicken and expand during the process. When all the butter has been worked into the custard, remove the bowl from the heat and cool over ice, whisking occasionally.

4 Whip the cream until thick and fold into the cooled custard to transform it into a mousse. Cover the mousse with plastic foodwrap and refrigerate until ready to use.

lemon verbena ice-cream

This is a fabulously refreshing ice-cream, the milk having been infused with the heady aroma of the leaves and flowers of lemon verbena. It is a must to make in summer when the plant becomes prolific. I also use the leaves as a base for tisane, a herbal tea that aids digestion. At the Restaurant we serve a slice of this ice-cream sandwiched between praline wafers – a play on the commercially produced Eskimo Pie. It is also wonderful served alongside the Lemon Tart (see page 103).

1 cup lemon verbena leaves, washed
500 ml milk
6 large egg yolks
200 g castor sugar
500 ml single (35%) cream

1 Infuse the lemon verbena leaves in the milk in a saucepan over very low heat for 2 hours, being careful not to reduce the volume of liquid.

2 Whisk the egg yolks and sugar together in a large bowl until pale and creamy.

3 Pour the hot milk through a fine-mesh sieve, discarding the leaves, and stir the scented milk into the eggs. Cook the milk mixture over a bain-marie on the stove until it reaches the consistency of custard, stirring constantly to keep smooth.

4 Pass the mixture through a fine-mesh sieve into another bowl and add the cream. Allow the mixture to cool completely.

5 Churn the cooled mixture in an ice-cream machine according to the manufacturer's instructions. Store in the freezer.

Serves 6

strawberry ice-cream

There is no substitute for good ice-cream. Fruit-based ice-cream should taste of fruit-enriched cream and not have ice splinters in it. This particular ice-cream does not have an egg custard base, giving it a more intense flavour. Use very ripe strawberries for the best results. The best way to purée strawberries is to blend them in a food processor.

250 ml strawberry purée
180 g castor sugar
25 ml lemon juice, strained
250 ml single (35%) cream

1 Pass the strawberry purée through a fine-mesh sieve to remove the seeds and give a finer texture. Mix the sugar and lemon juice into the purée thoroughly with a whisk.

2 Stir the cream into the mixture and churn in an ice-cream machine according to the manufacturer's instructions. Store in the freezer.

Serves 6

passionfruit ice-cream

Another perfect use for passionfruit, once again using the sieved juice to its best advantage. I incorporate the juice into the beaten egg yolk and sugar cold as I find the taste of the juice loses its intensity once it has been heated directly.

200 g castor sugar
6 egg yolks
500 ml single (35%) cream
250 ml passionfruit juice

1 Whisk the sugar and eggs together in a bowl until pale.

2 Heat half the cream in a saucepan to simmering point.

3 Stir the passionfruit juice into the egg mixture then pour in the hot cream, stirring well to incorporate, and cook over a bain-marie until the mixture is the consistency of custard. Remove from the heat and strain the custard through a fine-mesh sieve. Add the remaining cream to the custard and allow to cool.

4 Churn the mixture in an ice-cream machine according to the manufacturer's instructions. Store in the freezer.

Serves 6

Tropical Cassata Ice-cream

tropical cassata ice-cream

The ice-creams we serve at the Paramount tend to be spectacular, moulded affairs. Moulded ice-creams allow the eater to taste all the flavours with the scoop of a spoon, as well as providing a visual challenge, giving food a witty character and taking it beyond the ordinary. Making ice-cream at home does not need to involve this degree of detail as the moulds that are used in restaurants are often specially made. Get the flavours right and you can serve them as you wish. A simple layered effect, where you churn each flavour separately and lay one on top of the other in a plastic, rectangular storage container, works very well, and, when you turn it out, you can just slice and serve. Choose flavours that work together, that compliment each other. Make ice-cream in good quantities, perhaps layering some and leaving others plain. This way you always have a wonderful dessert to hand.

1 quantity of Strawberry Ice-cream (see page 125)
1 quantity of Passionfruit Ice-cream (see page 125)
1 quantity of Raspberry Sorbet (see page 123)
1 quantity of Pineapple Sorbet with Candied Fruit (see page 123)

1 Prepare one flavour of ice-cream at a time as directed. Divide between the desired number of containers and freeze.

2 When the first layer is frozen, prepare the next flavour as directed. Add a layer of ice-cream to the containers and freeze. Repeat this process with the remaining ice-cream.

3 Store the layered ice-cream in the freezer until required. To serve, unmould and cut into slices with a hot, sharp knife.

sauternes sabayon

A sabayon is a light custard that is whisked over heat – not stirred – making it very light and frothy. It needs to be served as soon as it is made. Use good quality sauternes in the cooking, one that you can drink with the dessert when it is made. As with all good cooking, quality ingredients give the best result. This is not a recipe for using up cheap wine.

500 ml single (35%) cream
250 ml sauternes
8 large egg yolks
150 g castor sugar

1 Heat the cream and sauternes in separate saucepans until simmering, making sure neither boils.

2 Whisk the egg yolks and sugar together in a bowl until light and fluffy. Pour the warm cream into the egg mixture in a slow, thin stream and whisk gently. Repeat the process with the warm sauternes.

3 Put the bowl over a simmering saucepan of water and whisk constantly until the mixture reaches the consistency of custard. Pass the sabayon through a fine-mesh sieve and use immediately.

chocolate cream meringues

A simple and satisfying petit four to make and serve with coffee. The meringues will keep in an airtight container for a week, just spread with the Chocolate Cream as you are ready to serve them.

3 egg whites
100 g castor sugar
100 g icing sugar, sifted
15 g cornflour
15 g cocoa powder
1 quantity of Chocolate Cream (see page 120)
extra cocoa

1 In an electric food mixer, beat the egg whites until stiff.

2 Gradually add the castor sugar in a thin, steady stream with the beaters at high speed. Fold in the sifted icing sugar, cornflour and cocoa.

3 Line a tray with baking paper and pipe on the meringue mixture in little peaked drops.

4 Leave in an oven set at 50°C until set, this takes about an hour.

5 To serve, sandwich 2 meringue drops together with Chocolate Cream. Dust with a little cocoa powder.

espresso ice-cream

The great flavour of this ice-cream relies on a base of strong, well-made espresso coffee. Do not be tempted to use an inferior instant substitute. I began making Espresso Ice-cream to accompany the Chocolate Mocha Tart (see page 131) as the textures and flavours work in perfect harmony. It remains a constant and popular feature on our menu.

500 ml single (35%) cream
250 ml milk
100 ml strong espresso coffee
25 ml coffee essence (preferably Trablit)
6 large egg yolks
200 g castor sugar
1 quantity of Chocolate Cream (see page 120)

1 In a saucepan, heat half the cream and the milk, coffee and coffee essence to simmering point.

2 Whisk the egg yolks and sugar in a large bowl until pale and creamy. Pour the hot cream over the eggs, whisking continuously, and cook over a bain-marie until the mixture is the consistency of custard. Pass the custard through a fine-mesh sieve and allow to cool.

3 Stir the remaining 250 ml of the cream into the cooled custard and churn in an ice-cream machine according to the manufacturer's instructions. Store in the freezer.

Serves 6

chocolate mocha tart with espresso ice-cream

Rich is an understatement when describing this double-layered tart. I believe when you use chocolate you should treat it as if you were an addict. Chocolate and moderation do not usually sit well together, so my chocolate desserts are designed for chocolate addicts – it's the full hit. When using chocolate in cooking, use the best couverture chocolate at your disposal, don't settle for low-grade cooking or compound chocolate as it just doesn't taste the same. The best brands are Callebaut (Belgian), Valrhona (French) and Lindt (Swiss). Start this recipe the day before you intend serving it as it needs time to set.
In the Restaurant we serve this tart with Espresso Ice-cream moulded into a spectacular cone shape. The ice-cream sits pointy end up alongside the sharp triangle of tart, making a strong geometric statement. See colour plate on page iii.

1 quantity of Chocolate Pastry (see page 91)
525 ml single (35%) cream
375 g dark couverture chocolate, in small pieces
30 ml coffee essence (preferably Trablit)
340 g milk chocolate, finely chopped
1 quantity of Espresso Ice-cream (see page 130)

1 Prepare the pastry according to the recipe. Bake in a 24 cm flan tin at 180°C for 12 minutes.

2 Bring 275 ml of the cream to simmering point in a saucepan.

3 Put the dark chocolate into a bowl and stir in the hot cream. Keep stirring until it has combined to form a ganache. Pour immediately into the freshly baked pastry shell. Refrigerate straight away and allow to set on an even surface for at least 4 hours.

4 Heat the remaining 250 ml of the cream and the coffee essence to simmering point and pour into a bowl over the milk chocolate and stir until smooth.

5 Remove the tart from the refrigerator and pour the mocha mixture over the dark chocolate layer, filling the tart right to the top of the pastry. Return it to the refrigerator to set firmly, about 3 hours. After the tart has set, cover with plastic foodwrap until ready to use.

6 To serve, unmould the tart and slice with a hot, sharp knife. Accompany it with a scoop of Espresso Ice-cream.

Serves 6

glazed nectarines with sauternes sabayon and toffee wafers

Make this dessert when nectarines are at their prime during summer. Select large, juicy, unblemished fruit to use for the cooking. The Toffee Wafers are much like brandy snaps, only they are smoothed out after cooking to remove their bubbly texture. The result is a smooth, thin wafer that resembles a shard. The wafers deteriorate quite quickly, especially in humid conditions, so be very organised when planning to make them and have a few practices beforehand so you become comfortable with the technique. The wafer mixture can be prepared and refrigerated up to 2 weeks in advance, leaving the cooking only for the day you require them.

9 ripe nectarines
50 g unsalted butter, diced
50 g castor sugar
1 quantity of Sauternes Sabayon (see page 128)

Toffee Wafers
50 g unsalted butter, softened
50 g castor sugar
2 egg whites
50 g plain flour

Toffee
100 g castor sugar
25 ml water

1 To make the Toffee Wafers, cream the butter and sugar in a bowl with an electric mixer until pale and creamy. This will take up to 10 minutes.

2 Fold the egg whites into the mixture a little at a time. Add the flour and work until the dough becomes smooth.

3 With a palette knife, spread a thin layer of the wafer mixture measuring 20 cm × 15 cm onto a buttered baking tray. Put the tray in the refrigerator until the mixture becomes firm, approximately 1 hour.

4 Preheat the oven to 180°C. Bake for 6 minutes until the mixture has set and is pale golden in colour. Remove from the oven. While the wafers are still warm, cut into 6 triangles that are 6 cm wide and 15 cm long. Work quickly to prevent fracturing, using a long-bladed sharp knife.

5 To make the Toffee, cook the sugar and water in a saucepan over a high heat until the mixture caramelises. Remove from the heat. Using a spoon, drizzle threads of toffee over the wafers.

6 Remove from the tray carefully with a flat slide and cool on a wire rack. Store in an airtight container between sheets of baking paper. The wafers are best used the same day as baked.

7 Cut the nectarines in half and remove the stones carefully, letting the fruit hold its shape. Place the nectarine halves on a baking tray, cut-side up, cover with butter cubes and sprinkle liberally with sugar. Grill until the sugar has caramelised and nectarines are glazed.

8 Put 3 nectarine halves into each bowl (flat soup bowls are best), pour over the warm sabayon and accompany with Toffee Wafers. Serve immediately.

Serves 6

toffee apple and vanilla cream tarts

With the preparation done beforehand, these tarts need only a few moments of your time when they are to be served. The tarts are more successful made individually as opposed to one big one as the Vanilla Cream is not made to be cut and hold its shape. The only trick is to have a blow torch on hand, easily acquired with refillable gas containers from any hardware shop for minimal cost. It works more effectively than a brulée iron in this instance and a griller will only heat the custard too much and cause it to separate and become runny.

½ quantity of Sweet Pastry (see page 89)
1 quantity of Thick Vanilla Cream (see page 120)
castor sugar

Toffee Apples
6 golden delicious apples, peeled and cored
100 ml water
500 g castor sugar

1 Prepare and bake 6 × 10 cm tart shells as directed.

2 To make the Toffee Apples, preheat the oven to 200°C. Cut the apples into eighths lengthwise.

3 Butter a baking dish and place the apple slices in a single layer over the base.

4 In a saucepan, bring the water and sugar to a boil and cook over a high heat until it forms a caramel. Pour over the apple.

5 Bake the apple for 7 minutes, then turn the slices over and cook for a further 5 minutes. Remove the apple from the tray while still warm and store on a sheet of baking paper until ready to use.

6 Cover the bases of the tart shells with the warm apple. Spoon over the Thick Vanilla Cream until each tart shell is full. Sprinkle the surface evenly with castor sugar and caramelise with a blow torch. Carefully remove the tarts from their tins and serve immediately.

Serves 6

poached peaches with raspberries and vanilla cream

Using the same flavours of the renowned Peach Melba in a different way, this is an easy dessert to assemble at the last minute provided the necessary preparation has been done. It captures the essence of summer when peaches and raspberries are plentiful and economical. I sometimes take these three flavours and turn them into ice-cream, mould them into layers and create a frozen Peach Melba slice. In this instance, the peach has been poached, the stone has been removed and the peach is then stuffed with raspberries and returned to its original shape.

250 ml sauternes
100 ml riesling
250 ml sugar syrup
25 ml vanilla essence
100 ml orange juice, strained
80 ml lemon juice, strained
zest of 1 orange
zest of 1 lemon
6 ripe yellow slipstone peaches
500 g raspberries
50 g castor sugar
1 quantity of Thick Vanilla Cream (see page 120)

1 In a stainless-steel braising pan, bring the sauternes, riesling, sugar syrup, vanilla, orange juice, 50 ml of the lemon juice and zests to a boil. Reduce to a simmer and add the peaches. Gently poach until the peaches are softened and the skins are just starting to split. Remove the peaches from the syrup and allow to cool. Reserve the syrup for another time (it keeps well refrigerated and with repeated use, the peach flavour intensifies).

2 Purée half the raspberries in a food processor or blender and pass the purée through a fine-mesh sieve to remove the seeds. Stir the sugar and remaining lemon juice into the raspberry purée until well mixed.

3 Peel the peaches and cut each one in half, removing the stones. Be careful not to rip the flesh – the peach halves should be perfectly intact and in shape.

4 Spread some raspberry purée on 6 serving plates and spoon a dollop of the Thick Vanilla Cream in the centre of the sauce.

5 Reassemble the peaches, stuffing some raspberries into the hollow where the stone was. Sit a 'whole' peach on top of the cream and dot a few extra raspberries around the peach on the cream and serve immediately.

Serves 6

honey bavarois with grilled figs and pistachio wafers

I always have this on the menu when figs are in season towards the end of summer and into autumn. The wafers will keep for a day in a sealed container away from heat and moisture.

12 ripe purple figs
icing sugar
1 quantity of Honey Bavarois (see page 122)
pistachio nuts, shelled and crushed

Pistachio Wafers
50 g castor sugar
50 g unsalted butter, softened
2 egg whites
50 g plain flour
25 g pistachio nuts, shelled and crushed

1 To make the Pistachio Wafers, put the sugar and butter into the bowl of an electric mixer and work on medium speed until the mixture is white and creamy, about 10 minutes.

2 Gradually add the egg whites to the creamed mixture and incorporate, then add the flour and work until the dough just comes together. Stir in the crushed nuts and refrigerate the mixture for 2 hours.

3 Preheat the oven to 140°C. For each biscuit, spread a tablespoon of the wafer mixture in a disc on a greased baking tray and bake for 5 minutes until cooked but not coloured.

4 Remove the tray from the oven and, working quickly, remove the biscuit from the tray with a spatula and roll up into a thin cigar shape while the biscuit is still hot, so that it sets into its shape. Allow to cool, then store in an airtight container.

5 Just before serving, cut the figs in half lengthwise and dust liberally with icing sugar. Grill for 2–3 minutes until glazed.

6 Turn out each bavarois onto a serving plate. Place 4 fig halves around the base of each bavarois and serve with a Pistachio Wafer. Sprinkle some extra crushed pistachio nuts on top of the bavarois.

Serves 6

shortbread biscuits with lime mousse and mango

The buttery nature of these biscuits is offset by the tartness and acidity of the Lime Mousse, which in turn is balanced with the sweetness of the ripe mango – the whole bringing to mind edible tropical pleasures. A dessert to have when mangoes are at their best. The biscuits can be stored in a sealed container between layers of baking paper until needed. They are best used the same day they are baked.

1 quantity of Shortbread Pastry (see page 90)
3 mangoes
1 quantity of Lime Mousse (see page 124)
icing sugar

Lime Syrup
50 ml water
250 g castor sugar
3 limes

1 To make the biscuits, roll the pastry out on a cool, floured surface until it is 5 mm thick. Using a 7 cm pastry cutter with a fluted edge, cut out 12 pastries, arrange on a baking tray and refrigerate for 15 minutes.

2 Preheat the oven to 150°C. Bake the biscuits for 6 minutes until firm but not coloured. When the biscuits are cooked, slide them off the baking tray with a spatula onto a wire rack and leave to set for at least 5 minutes.

3 To make the Lime Syrup, boil the water and sugar in a saucepan over a high heat until the mixture forms a pale caramel.

4 Juice and zest the limes and add to the caramel. Cook over a medium heat for a further 15 minutes until it becomes a syrup. Pour the syrup into a stainless steel bowl to stop the cooking process and allow to cool completely before using.

5 Just before serving, slice the cheeks off the mangoes, remove the skin and cut each piece into thin slices.

6 To assemble, spoon some mousse onto each plate over an area a little smaller than one of the biscuits, top with mango, drizzle a little syrup around it and finish off with a shortbread biscuit. Carefully build a second layer on top of the biscuit – first the lime mousse and then some more mango slices and finally another biscuit dusted with icing sugar. Serve immediately.

Serves 6

soft meringue, passionfruit and strawberry roulade

This recipe reworks the very Australian image of the pavlova into a more refined presentation that still captures the flavours and textures of the original form. It is a great standby because it can literally be thrown together in no time, looks spectacular and provides a big impact without impinging on your time when it comes to serving. It's what I call an easy 'slice and serve' dessert. You can adjust the filling according to the season, vary the fruit you use and substitute whipped cream or mascarpone for the Passionfruit Cream. Apply the same principle and make it in summer or for Christmas using mascarpone, cherries, blackberries and lychees.

hazelnut oil
8 egg whites
375 g castor sugar
2 teaspoons vanilla essence
2 teaspoons white vinegar
2 teaspoons cornflour
sifted icing sugar
1 quantity of Passionfruit Cream (see page 120)
500 g strawberries, sliced
2 tablespoons passionfruit pulp

1 Preheat the oven to 160°C. Line a 4 cm deep, 24 cm × 32 cm baking tin with baking paper and lightly grease the paper with hazelnut oil.

2 Beat the egg whites until stiff peaks form. Gradually add the sugar while still beating until the mixture is thick and glossy. Fold in the vanilla, vinegar and cornflour. Spread the meringue into the prepared tin with a spatula, level it off and bake for 20 minutes.

3 Allow the meringue to cool in the tin for a few minutes after removing it from the oven. Turn the meringue out onto a sheet of baking paper that has been dusted with the icing sugar. Allow to cool for 10 minutes.

4 Spread the meringue with the Passionfruit Cream, add half the strawberries and roll up carefully into a roulade using the paper to keep a firm shape. Refrigerate on a baking tray for 3 hours.

5 To serve, slice the roulade into portions and top with the remaining strawberries, drizzle with passionfruit pulp and dust with icing sugar.

Serves 6

Fruit Jellies and Preserves

This chapter is a dedication to the seasonal abundance of fruits that demand we make the most of their perfect ripeness, perfume and flavour and allow them to endure for as long as possible in a suspended preserved state. The art of preservation arrests the process of decay and gives us greater flexibility in our cooking and eating choices and goes beyond the boundaries of limited availability. Although economy plays an important role in the preserving process, it is often the way the ripe 'at-its-peak' fruit is transformed into an even more sensuous and appealing product that gives us the desire to adopt this practice. Summer, in particular, is a time of abundance and we have to work hard to capture the essence and seductive flavours of the heat so we can relive them in the colder, leaner months of winter.

Fruit can be preserved in its original shape steeped in an alcoholic sugar syrup or it can be candied, while over-ripe fruit can be juiced to flavour drinks, syrups and sauces that may accompany other fruit or dessert items. Sugar acts in the same way as salt in the preservation process: it inhibits the growth of bacteria when used in a concentrated form. It also acts as a setting agent, along with the natural acid and pectin found in varying degrees in fruit. The amount of sugar needed is determined by the type of preserve you are making. Fruit 'cheeses' and pastes use more sugar than fruit butters, which in turn use more sugar than jams and jellies.

Preserving all types of food items in the Restaurant has enabled a greater flexibility in our menu-planning decisions, giving us a wider scope and understanding of the science of food. I always question opening a can if I can make it, an important legacy from my days of working at Oasis Seros. I am helping to pass that skill and practice on to the people who work with me in my kitchen now. Preserving is a time-honoured tradition that appears to be disappearing with the advent of fast and frozen food and the modern desire for immediate gratification. It is important, then, that we maintain the skills of food preservation, to be reminded of the source, to respect the produce and the process, even if we don't necessarily do it ourselves. You don't have to go overboard and preserve everything in sight, just use a little of your time occasionally to indulge in the very gratifying experience of prolonging the life of our natural resources.

With all preserving and dessert work, it is imperative that you use only stainless steel or copper equipment to prevent tarnishing and the fruit discolouring. While you are about it, buy a jelly bag, or muslin, some preserving jars and a confectionery thermometer. Don't forget to label your produce – or eat it!

We stock all the preserves mentioned in this chapter at the Store when that particular fruit is in season. I use the preserves throughout the year when planning menus – they are indispensable!

apple jelly

Apples are high in natural pectin, a setting agent necessary for making jelly. Firm red or pink apples give the best flavour and colour to the jelly. Often, apples are added to other fruits when making jellies to give enough pectin for the jelly to reach setting point.

5 kg red apples (preferably Tasmanian pink lady or New Zealand gala)
5 kg castor sugar
2 litres apple juice
1 stick cinnamon

1 Wash the apples thoroughly. Roughly chop the apples and put them into a large stockpot with their peel, cores and seeds.

2 Add the remaining ingredients to the stockpot and bring to a boil gently. Cook over a moderate heat until the apple is very soft.

3 Pour the contents of the stockpot into a prepared jelly bag, or several layers of muslin, that has been suspended over a large bowl or bucket and allow the juices to drain overnight.

4 Tie the muslin or jelly bag to a wooden spoon and twist the spoon around gently to extract as much juice as possible.

5 Pour the strained juices into a large, clean pot and bring to a boil. Cook over moderate heat until it reaches setting point (110°C). To check whether the jelly stage has been reached, test the syrup on the back of a cold spoon.

6 Ladle the jelly into hot, sterilised preserving jars and seal.

apple butter

This recipe works best with tart, green cooking apples to balance the added sweetness. It is delicious spread on toast or brioche or served warm with apple tea cake and lashings of cream.

2 kg granny smith apples
350 ml apple juice
250 g brown sugar
seeds of 4 cardamom pods, ground
1 teaspoon ground cinnamon
½ teaspoon freshly grated nutmeg
1 teaspoon lemon zest, minced

1 Roughly chop the apples, including the peel and cores.

2 In a large stockpot, bring the chopped apple and apple juice to a boil over gentle heat. Stir regularly to prevent sticking.

3 Pour the contents of the stockpot into a conical sieve over another pot and press the solids through the sieve. Discard the contents of the sieve and gently reheat the apple purée with the sugar, spices and zest.

4 Simmer the apple mixture for 50 minutes or until thickened. Ladle the Apple Butter into hot, sterilised preserving jars and seal.

5 Store in the refrigerator.

grape jellies

Make this delicate jelly in individual moulds when grapes are at their best. Don't try using a large mould as the jelly won't set.

1 kg muscat grapes
150 g castor sugar
50 ml liqueur muscat
50 ml lemon juice, strained
4 gelatine leaves
48 seedless green grapes, peeled

1 In a pan, bring the muscat grapes, sugar and liqueur to a boil, then reduce the heat and simmer until the grapes just lose their shape, about 15 minutes.

2 Pass the grapes through a fine-mesh sieve, pressing firmly to extract as much liquid as possible. You should have 750 ml of grape juice. Add the lemon juice.

3 Dissolve the gelatine leaves in cold water until softened. Squeeze out the water and stir into the hot grape juice until the gelatine has dissolved. Strain the grape juice again and allow the mixture to cool slightly.

4 Divide the peeled grapes between 6 individual jelly moulds and pour over the grape liquid. Allow to set in the refrigerator until firm.

5 Turn out the jellies and serve immediately.

Serves 6

quince jelly

The quince is a native of Persia (modern-day Iran), a hot barren land, and is common in Middle Eastern and North African cooking. Readily available at fruit markets just as the summer fruits are fading, quinces come into their own in savoury and sweet cooking (they require treatment before they can be eaten). For further information, refer either to Maggie Beer's Maggie's Farm *or Jane Grigson's* Fruit Book, *both of which include evocative chapters about the virtues of the quince. Like the apple, it is high in natural pectin, so making jelly is quite easy.*

2 kg ripe quinces
4 litres water
castor sugar
250 ml lemon juice

1 Chop the quinces, including the peel and cores, and put them in a large stockpot with the water and cook over a moderate heat until the fruit is very soft.

2 Pour the contents of the stockpot into a prepared jelly bag, or layers of muslin, that is suspended over a bucket or bowl and allow the juices to drain overnight. Do not press or force the juices through the bag, as doing so will make the jelly cloudy.

3 Measure the strained juice with a cup measure, then transfer it to a clean, large saucepan and add an equal amount of sugar. Cook over a low heat – but do not let it boil – until the sugar has dissolved.

4 Stir in the lemon juice and increase the heat until the mixture boils. Skim and continue to boil for 15 minutes or until it reaches setting point (110°C). To check whether the jelly stage has been reached, test the syrup on the back of a cold spoon.

5 Ladle the jelly into hot, sterilised preserving jars and seal.

quince marmalade

A wickedly good and unusual preserve to make and have on hand when quinces are in abundance.

2 kg ripe quinces
500 ml water
500 g castor sugar
75 ml lemon juice, strained

1 Chop half the quinces, including the peel and cores, and put them into a large stainless steel stockpot with the water and bring to a boil over a low heat. Simmer for 30 minutes or until the fruit is very soft.

2 Tip the contents of the stockpot into a prepared jelly bag, or layers of muslin, that is suspended over a bucket or large bowl and let it drain for 12 hours or overnight. Do not press or force the juices through as doing so will make the jelly cloudy.

3 Combine the juices from the bucket with the sugar in a clean, large pot and cook over a low heat, stirring frequently until the sugar has dissolved.

4 While the mixture is cooking slowly, peel and core the remaining quinces and slice the fruit into thin shreds. You may need to keep the quince in acidulated water until ready to use to stop it discolouring.

5 Bring the syrup in the pot to a boil, add the shredded quince and lemon juice. Return to a simmer and continue to cook gently until the fruit is cooked, skimming any froth from the surface regularly. Bring the syrup back to a boil and continue to cook until setting point (110°C) is reached. To check whether the jelly stage has been reached, test the syrup on the back of a cold spoon.

6 Ladle the marmalade into hot, sterilised preserving jars and seal.

seville orange marmalade

This jam is an adaptation of the St Benoit Three-day Marmalade in Jane Grigson's Fruit Book. *Navel or valencia oranges can also be used, but the particular tartness and flavour of the seville oranges give the jam a distinctive character. They are only available for a short time in early summer so look out for them or find someone who has a tree. When they are available, blood oranges also make a wonderful jam with this recipe. If using any other orange than the seville, you would need to add a lemon to the recipe, treated in the same way as the oranges.*

10 seville oranges
castor sugar

1 Slice the oranges into thin rounds, discarding the ends. Remove the seeds and tie in a muslin bag.

2 Place the fruit and seeds in a large bowl or bucket and soak in enough water to cover, with a weight on top, for 24 hours.

3 Put the fruit, seeds and the water into a large stockpot and gently bring to a boil. Simmer for 1 hour and skim the surface with a mesh spoon to remove any scum that forms. Turn the heat off, allow to cool, then cover the stockpot and leave to sit for another 24 hours.

4 Measure the contents of the stockpot and for every kilogram of fruit and juice, add 1.25 kg castor sugar.

5 Bring the fruit and sugar to a boil in a clean, large pot and continue to boil gently, stirring occasionally, until the marmalade reaches setting point (110°C). This will take about 1 hour. To check whether the jelly stage has been reached, test the syrup on the back of a cold spoon.

6 Remove the muslin bag and ladle the marmalade into hot, sterilised jars and seal.

cumquat marmalade

This small oval fruit, with its sweet-and-sour characteristic, is a member of the citrus family and perfect to preserve as it is edible in its entirety.

2 kg cumquats
castor sugar

1 Cut the cumquats in half and remove the seeds. Put the seeds in a muslin bag and tie up.

2 Weigh the cumquats, put them in a bucket, cover with water and refrigerate overnight.

3 Transfer the cumquats, water and seeds to a large, heavy-based stockpot and add sugar to half the weight of the cumquats. Bring the stockpot to a boil and simmer for 1 hour. Turn off the heat and allow to stand overnight.

4 Bring the stockpot to a boil again and cook the marmalade until it reaches setting point (110°C). To check whether jelly stage has been reached, test the syrup on the back of a cold spoon.

5 Ladle the marmalade into hot, sterilised jars and seal.

brandied peaches

Keep the taste of summer alive by preserving peaches when they are in peak season towards the end of summer. You can use them in winter in a trifle, baked in cakes, made into puddings or topped with a crumble. These peaches keep well for a few months.

750 ml sauternes
250 ml riesling
1 litre sugar syrup
1 vanilla pod, split open
16 ripe yellow slipstone peaches, washed
750 ml brandy

1 In a wide-based braising pan, bring the sauternes, riesling, sugar syrup and vanilla pod to a boil and cook for 30 minutes on a gentle boil.

2 Reduce the heat to low, add the peaches and poach very gently for 10 minutes, turning them regularly in the syrup. Remove the peaches from the syrup, allow to cool enough to handle, then peel.

3 Add the brandy to the syrup and remove the vanilla pod.

4 Sterilise 2 × 2 litre preserving jars. Put 8 peaches in each one and pour the hot syrup over until the peaches are covered, then seal.

muscat-poached fruit

Dried fruit is available all year round and by preparing it this way you have a ready-made fruit dessert during the winter months when many varieties of fruit are not in season. Choose fruit that has been recently dried; it will be soft and malleable and taste fresh. Fruit from Australia's riverland is usually of the best quality. Serve this wonderful concoction warm, with clotted cream and toasted fruit bread.

750 ml liqueur muscat
250 ml water
500 g castor sugar
1 vanilla pod, split open
6 dried figs
12 dried apricots
8 dried peaches
6 prunes, pitted
4 dried pineapple rings, quartered
½ cup dried cherries

1 Boil the liqueur, water, sugar and vanilla pod in a large saucepan over a high heat for 20 minutes until the liquid begins to thicken and become syrupy.

2 Reduce the heat and add all the fruit. Simmer for 20 minutes until the fruit is tender and the syrup has reduced slightly. Stir regularly to distribute the fruit evenly in the syrup.

3 Store in a sealed container in the refrigerator.

preserved cherries

Cherries have a very short season around Christmas in Australia, but their shelf life can be extended by preserving them for later use whenever you have the desire to indulge in their taste.

1 litre sugar syrup
400 ml cherry liqueur or cherry brandy
1 stick cinnamon
3 pieces whole dried mace
2 kg black ron cherries, pitted

1 In a large, wide-based stockpot, bring the sugar syrup, liqueur, cinnamon and mace to a boil and simmer for 20 minutes.

2 Add the cherries and simmer gently for 15 minutes, stirring occasionally. Spoon the cherries and their syrup into hot, sterilised jars and seal.

3 Store refrigerated until ready to use.

spiced plums

These plums are very versatile. Used as they are, they make a warming winter dessert; cooked until the fruit has broken down, then sieved, these spicy plums make a sauce that can be preserved in hot, sterilised jars.

2 litres water
2 kg castor sugar
200 ml brandy
300 ml cassis
1 vanilla pod, split open
2 sticks cinnamon
6 cloves
3 pieces whole dried mace
3 kg satsuma or blood plums, washed

1 Put all the ingredients except the plums in a large stockpot and bring to a boil. Simmer for 20 minutes.

2 Add the plums to the syrup and simmer gently for 10 minutes until the plums are softened but not broken down. Pour the plums and their syrup into hot, sterilised preserving jars and seal.

3 When cool, refrigerate and store for 1 month before using. Peel the plums when ready to use.

steamed cumquat sponge puddings with orange sabayon

The construction and gentle steaming of these puddings makes them feathery light. A good balance of fruit acid and sugar, they show off the prepared cumquats to their best advantage.

3 large (61 g) eggs, separated
150 g castor sugar
2 teaspoons Cointreau
30 ml orange-flower water
190 ml milk
1 tablespoon melted butter
280 g self-raising flour, sifted
6 tablespoons Cumquat Marmalade (see page 148)

Orange Sabayon
250 ml single (35%) cream
50 ml milk
zest of 2 oranges
4 egg yolks
75 g castor sugar
75 ml orange juice, strained
15 ml Cointreau
15 ml orange-flower water

1 Preheat the oven to 180°C.

2 Cream the egg yolks and sugar in an electric food mixer until pale and foamy. With the beaters on medium speed, add the Cointreau, orange-flower water and milk, then the butter. Stir in the sifted flour gently.

3 Whisk the egg whites until stiff, then fold into the batter.

4 Butter and sugar 6 × 8 cm wide pudding moulds that are 5 cm deep. Spoon the marmalade into the bases of the moulds and pour in the pudding mixture. Stand the moulds in a baking dish and pour in water to come halfway up the sides of the moulds. Cover with foil and cook for 30 minutes, rotating the moulds at 15 minutes to ensure even cooking.

5 While the puddings are cooking, make the Orange Sabayon. Heat the cream, milk and zest together over a low heat until simmering. Whisk the egg yolks and sugar together in a bowl until pale and foamy. Whisk in the orange juice, Cointreau and orange-flower water.

6 Strain the hot cream, discarding the zest, and whisk into the eggs and continue to cook and whisk over a bain-marie until the mixture reaches the consistency of a light and fluffy custard.

7 Remove the moulds from the water bath and allow to cool slightly. Run a small knife around the edges to loosen the moulds and turn out onto serving plates. Serve immediately with the hot Orange Sabayon.

Serves 6

apple butter galette

This is a melt-in-the-mouth, light-as-a-feather dessert. It has to be eaten as soon as it is baked, as reheating makes it soggy. Have the pastry rounds, apple slices and Apple Butter ready and you will be able to whip this up in no time.

1 quantity of Puff Pastry (see page 92)
3 golden delicious apples
6 tablespoons Apple Butter (see page 143)
castor sugar
icing sugar

1 Preheat the oven to 200°C. Roll out the pastry and cut 6 rounds 15 cm in diameter. Refrigerate until required.

2 Peel, core and cut the apples into thin segments.

3 Arrange the pastry rounds on a buttered baking tray and spread with the Apple Butter. Fan the apple slices over the butter, working from the centre out. Sprinkle with castor sugar and bake for 12 minutes until golden.

4 Dust the hot pastries with icing sugar and serve with a rich vanilla or caramel ice-cream.

Serves 6

baked plum and hazelnut crumble

This is one of those heart-warming desserts to indulge in on a cold night by the fire. It takes little time to put together and is served in the gratin dish it is baked in, so really requires no last-minute fuss or bother. One large crumble can be made instead of individual ones, if desired.

24 Spiced Plums (see page 151)
100 g brioche crumbs
125 g plain flour
100 g unsalted butter, softened
75 g hazelnuts, roasted and ground
1 teaspoon ground cinnamon
100 g castor sugar

1 Preheat the oven to 200°C.

2 Peel the plums, cut them in half and remove the stones. Arrange the plums in individual buttered gratin dishes and spoon a small amount of their syrup over them.

3 In a bowl, work together the other ingredients by hand until the mixture resembles wet breadcrumbs. Spoon the crumble mix evenly over the plums.

4 Place the gratin dishes on a baking tray and bake for 12 minutes until the crumble is golden. Serve hot with clotted or thick cream.

Serves 6

brandied peach and raspberry trifle with vanilla cream

This is a favourite dessert served in late summer when the fruit is abundant and at its best.

6 slices Génoise Sponge (see page 158)
6 Brandied Peaches (see page 149)
500 g raspberries
12 tablespoons Thick Vanilla Cream (see page 120)
6 tablespoons thick (45%) cream, whipped

1 Line the bases of 6 trifle dishes with the cake and soak with some of the brandy syrup from the peaches.

2 Slice the peaches and arrange them on top of the cake. Add a few raspberries, fill the dishes with the vanilla cream and cover with the whipped cream. Top with more raspberries and serve.

Serves 6

baked quinces with quince marmalade brioche and cream

Our cool room is stocked with ripe quinces for a good three months of the year, giving off their heavenly, musky sweet aroma, waiting to be transformed into syrup, pickle, jam, jelly, marmalade or paste to serve with cheese or just poached in sugar syrup until they become deep-red and luscious. Because of their less than-appealing raw state, quinces, often referred to as the fruit of love, have been largely overlooked, but when treated with the respect they deserve, they rise to the challenge and win over your tastebuds.

1 quantity of Brioche Dough (see page 95)
6 tablespoons Quince Marmalade (see page 146)
3 large, ripe quinces
6 tablespoons clotted cream, crème fraîche or fromage blanc

Quince Syrup
4 ripe quinces
castor sugar
1 stick cinnamon
1 vanilla pod, split open

1 To make the Quince Syrup, chop the quinces coarsely, including the peel, core and seeds, and weigh. Put the chopped quince into a large stockpot with an equal weight of sugar and enough water to cover. Add the cinnamon stick and the vanilla pod.

2 Bring the stockpot to a boil and cook on a medium heat for 2 hours or until the fruit becomes a dark, rich red colour and the liquid has become syrupy. Strain the syrup through a fine-mesh sieve or piece of muslin, pressing to extract as much liquid as possible. Discard the pulp.

3 Prepare the brioche as directed. Roll the dough out into a 40 cm × 25 cm rectangle and spread the marmalade over the surface. Roll up into a long sausage, like a roulade, and rest the dough on a baking tray on its seam to rise in a warm, draught-free place for 20 minutes until it has doubled in volume.

4 Preheat the oven to 220°C. Bake the brioche for 40 minutes. Turn out to cool on a wire rack and reduce the oven temperature to 150°C.

5 Peel and core the quinces, then cut into quarters.

6 Bring the Quince Syrup to a boil in a wide-based, ovenproof pan, add the quinces and cover with a lid. Be careful not to boil the syrup or the fruit will break up and lose its shape. Bake the quinces in the syrup slowly for 4 hours or until they are cooked and a deep-red colour. The longer and slower the cooking, the better. (The quinces can be stored in the syrup once they have cooked until they are ready to be used. If that is the case, reheat them gently in their syrup on low heat.)

7 Cut the brioche into 4 cm thick slices and, when ready to serve, toast lightly on each side.

8 Sit the brioche slices on serving plates and top with the cooked quinces, strained from their liquid (reserve the syrup for future quince cooking). Spoon a little Quince Syrup around and serve with clotted cream, crème fraîche or fromage blanc.

Serves 6

chocolate sponge and orange marmalade puddings with chocolate jaffa sauce

This is a great winter dessert, classic in its combination of chocolate and orange and foolproof (almost) in its method. An interesting alternative to the predictable use of marmalade. One large pudding can be made instead of individual ones, if desired.

12 tablespoons Seville Orange Marmalade (see page 147)
100 g dark couverture chocolate
6 large (61 g) eggs, separated
100 g castor sugar
1 teaspoon Cointreau or Grand Marnier liqueur
100 g blanched almonds, ground
50 g fine, fresh brioche crumbs or breadcrumbs

Chocolate Jaffa Sauce
400 ml single (35%) cream
75 g castor sugar
75 ml orange syrup
25 ml Cointreau or Grand Marnier liqueur
250 g dark couverture chocolate

1 Preheat the oven to 180°C.

2 To prepare the puddings, butter and sugar 6 individual pudding moulds. Spoon 1 tablespoon of the marmalade into the base of each prepared mould.

3 Melt the chocolate in a bowl over a bain-marie and allow to cool slightly.

4 Whisk the egg yolks with half the sugar in a bowl until they foam. Stir the liqueur and then the chocolate into the egg mixture.

5 Beat the egg whites until firm, then gradually add the remaining sugar and beat until stiff. Fold the egg whites into the chocolate base with a whisk, keeping the mixture as aerated as possible, and then add the almonds and the brioche crumbs or breadcrumbs.

6 Pour the mixture into the prepared moulds and stand these in a baking dish. Pour in water to come halfway up the sides of the moulds, cover loosely with buttered foil and bake for 30 minutes. Test with a skewer in the centre – if it comes out clean the puddings are ready. (One larger pudding will take longer to cook than the individual ones.)

7 While the puddings are cooking, make the Chocolate Jaffa Sauce. In a saucepan, bring the cream, sugar, syrup and liqueur to simmering point.

8 Shave the chocolate with a knife, place in a bowl and pour over the hot cream. Stir to combine. Use immediately or reheat gently later over a bain-marie.

9 When the puddings are cooked, uncover and lift out of the water bath carefully.

10 To serve, turn the cooked puddings out of their moulds carefully, running a small knife around the edges to loosen them. Heat the extra marmalade and spoon over the tops of the puddings and pour the warm chocolate sauce around their bases.

Serves 6

muscat-poached fruit with meringue, praline and clotted cream

This dessert is an interpretation of the Gaudi architecture in Barcelona. The meringue structure hides the fruit and cream filling from the initial glance but once the wall is broken, the soft and sweet centre is revealed. I enjoy the challenge of creating a visual impact with desserts without being fussy, tricked-up or using unnecessary garnish. The essential flavours should be the strength behind the appearance – you can't have one without the other.

6 tablespoons clotted cream
6 tablespoons Muscat-poached Fruit (see page 150)

Meringue Cones
3 egg whites
100 g castor sugar
100 g icing sugar
15 g cornflour

Praline
300 g castor sugar
50 ml water
hazelnut oil
250 g hazelnuts, roasted and skinned

1 To make the Meringue Cones, whisk the egg whites until stiff and gradually whisk in the sugar. The whites must hold their stiffness and body at this stage so they don't collapse on the moulds.

2 Sift the icing sugar and cornflour together and gently stir into the egg whites. Spoon the meringue mixture into a piping bag.

3 Line 6 × 10 cm high conical moulds with baking paper, folding the excess paper into the hollow centre to secure. Pipe the meringue onto the moulds in upward, even strokes, working from the bottom up, finishing each time with a flick of the wrist so the meringue forms a spiked peak. Make sure each line joins the next, so there are no gaps.

4 Put the Meringue Cones on a tray lined with baking paper and sit in a 50°C oven for 8 hours or until cooked and firm but not coloured. Remove the meringues carefully from their moulds and store upright in an airtight container until ready to use.

5 To make the Praline, boil the sugar and water in a saucepan over a high heat until the mixture becomes a pale caramel colour.

6 Oil a bench or marble slab with hazelnut oil and sit the nuts on it. Pour the hot caramel over the nuts and allow it to cool. Scrape the toffeed nuts off the bench with a spatula and keep stored in an airtight container in the refrigerator. When you need some praline, process small amounts of the toffeed nuts in a food processor or mortar and pestle until it forms a fine crumb.

7 To assemble, hold the meringues upside-down and spoon in a little clotted cream, then fill with the muscat fruit. Add a spoonful of cream to seal the bottom of each cone and turn up onto a serving plate. Sit a few pieces of the fruit on the tops of the meringues and drizzle over some of the fruit syrup. Sprinkle with praline and serve immediately.

Serves 6

passionfruit miroir

Passionfruit has an appropriate name. I am passionate about them. The fruit is always on the menu in some form or another. Just as any self-respecting dessert list has a chocolate item, mine also has passionfruit. When they are plentiful and cheap, we make litres and litres of juice that we freeze for making ice-cream, sorbet and curd at a later date.
If the Chocolate Mocha Tart is for the chocolate addict, this is the dessert for the passionfruit addict, as it involves layers of different passionfruit-flavoured textures; its name derived from the clarity of the jelly layer that has the appearance of a mirror. The Génoise sponge used here is wonderfully versatile and freezes well. When preparing the Passionfruit Bavarois (see page 122), keep the mixture in a large bowl until it is required rather than making individual bowls.

1 quantity of Passionfruit Bavarois (see page 122)
pulp of 3 passionfruit

Génoise Sponge
5 large (61 g) eggs, separated
150 g castor sugar
150 g plain flour, sifted
1 teaspoon vanilla essence
50 g unsalted butter, melted

Passionfruit Syrup
300 g castor sugar
100 ml water
250 ml passionfruit juice

Passionfruit Jelly
90 ml passionfruit juice
90 ml sugar syrup
1½ gelatine leaves

1 To make the Génoise Sponge, preheat the oven to 160°C. Whisk the egg yolks and sugar in a bowl until pale and creamy. Add the flour, vanilla and melted butter and stir to incorporate.

2 Whisk the egg whites until stiff and gently fold into the cake batter. Pour the batter into a greased 24 cm square cake tin and bake for 20 minutes or until cooked. Test by inserting a skewer into the centre; if it comes out clean, the cake is cooked. Turn the cake out onto a wire rack to cool.

3 To make the Passionfruit Syrup, bring the sugar and water to a boil in a stainless steel saucepan and continue to cook rapidly until the syrup becomes a pale caramel. Add the passionfruit juice, reduce the heat and simmer for 10 minutes. Cool the syrup completely before serving.

4 To make the Passionfruit Jelly, bring the passionfruit juice and sugar syrup to a boil in a saucepan.

5 Soak the gelatine leaves in cold water until softened, then squeeze out the water and stir into the hot juice until the gelatine has dissolved. Pass the syrup through a fine-mesh sieve and allow to cool.

6 To assemble the miroirs, spoon the Passionfruit Jelly just as it begins to set into the bases of 6 plastic dariole moulds 8 cm in diameter so that it is 3 mm thick. Refrigerate until set.

7 Spoon the bavarois on top of the jelly, filling the moulds until 5 mm from the top. Refrigerate until set.

8 Cut the cake into 6 × 8 cm rounds that are 5 mm thick. Position the cake bases on top of the bavarois and cover with plastic foodwrap and refrigerate until ready to serve.

9 When ready to serve, hold the plastic moulds in hot water for a few seconds to loosen them and turn out onto serving plates. Spoon some fresh passionfruit pulp that has been mixed with some Passionfruit Syrup around each miroir.

Serves 6

Passionfruit Miroir

cherry almond cake

This cake features regularly on the Store menu when cherries abound and stays there until the cherry preserves have been used and we have to wait for the next season. It is a very moist cake and keeps well for 3 days in a sealed container.

250 g unsalted butter
500 g castor sugar
6 large (61 g) eggs
1 teaspoon vanilla essence
400 g plain flour
1 teaspoon baking powder
200 g ground blanched almonds
185 g crème fraîche or sour cream
400 g strained Preserved Cherries (see page 151)

1 Preheat the oven to 180°C.

2 Cream the butter and sugar in an electric mixer until pale and creamy. With the beaters at high speed, add the eggs, one at a time, then the vanilla.

3 Sift the flour and baking powder and add to the egg mixture with the ground almonds. Beat for a couple of minutes on medium speed. Add the crème fraîche and beat gently until incorporated. Stir in the cherries by hand.

4 Spoon the mixture into a 24 cm round cake tin that has been greased with butter and then coated with sugar. Bake for 55–60 minutes until golden. Test with a skewer; if it comes out clean the cake is cooked.

5 Serve with some of the cherry syrup and extra crème fraîche.

cherry brioche with cherry syrup

One of my favourite ways of serving brioche is to laden the dough with fruit for sweetness and built-in flavour. There's nothing better than the seductive aroma and taste of fruit brioche served hot from the oven with cream or mascarpone.

1 quantity of Brioche Dough (see page 95)
12 tablespoons strained Preserved Cherries (see page 151)
500 ml syrup from the Preserved Cherries
icing sugar

1 Prepare the brioche as directed. When it is ready to be kneaded, work 6 tablespoons of the cherries into the dough.

2 Butter and sugar a large brioche mould and place the dough in it, adding a little ball of dough on top as in the classic presentation. Allow the dough to rise in the mould for 20 minutes, then bake in a 200°C oven for 40 minutes with a water bath on the shelf beneath.

3 Turn out the freshly baked brioche and dust with icing sugar. Bring the syrup to a boil in a saucepan and allow to reduce to 300 ml. Stir in the remaining cherries, heat through and pour around the brioche.

Glossary

The following ingredients and processes are used throughout this book and may not be familiar to all readers. You will find among them preparations requiring attention before it is possible to proceed with some of the recipes. Many of these are store-cupboard items – always have them on hand and you'll cut your preparation time significantly. I suggest that you familiarise yourself with the contents of the Glossary before you start cooking and stock up on the more frequently used items.

For ease of reading, recipes for the stocks I recommend using can be found at the end of the Glossary.

References to other Glossary entries are indicated by the use of SMALL CAPITALS.

acidulated water Water to which lemon juice has been added. Cut fruit or vegetables are immersed in acidulated water to prevent browning.

bain-marie A saucepan half-filled with water kept at simmering point over which a stainless steel bowl fits comfortably. The water must not touch the bowl. A bain-marie is used for gentle cooking.

bake blind To prevent shrinkage during cooking, baking paper is placed over prepared pastry and weighed down with dried beans, rice or pastry weights. When the pastry has been cooked, the paper and weights are removed and kept for future use.

bavarois moulds *see* dessert moulds

beef stock *see* page 164

belacan A compressed shrimp paste of Malaysian origin, belacan is called *trasi* in Indonesia, *kapi* in Thailand and *mam ruoc* in Vietnam. Shrimp are salted and fermented in the sun, then mashed into a paste. Don't be put off by the smell; when DRY-ROASTED and crumbled belacan gives a complexity to the flavour of the food to which it is added. I prefer the Malaysian variety. It is sold in blocks and is dark-brown, almost black. It keeps indefinitely but, once opened, should be kept very well wrapped in a container in the refrigerator.

candlenut A soft nut with a similar appearance to the macadamia. Very rich in oil, it is used as a thickening agent in laksa pastes and curries. The packet is best kept in the refrigerator once opened. Available from Asian food stores.

capsicums, roasting To prepare, cut blemish-free capsicums into quarters lengthwise. Remove the seeds and membrane, arrange skin-side up on a baking tray and place under a hot grill or salamander. Allow the skin to blacken and blister, then put the charred capsicum in a plastic bag to sweat for a few minutes. When cool enough to handle, peel off the blackened skin, wash off any other black bits, if necessary, and slice lengthwise into strips. Store in a jar, covered with virgin olive oil, until ready to use. Keeps for about 8 days, refrigerated.

cardamom, black A larger pod than the more common green cardamom, with a hard brown shell that is filled with seeds used in cooking to tenderise meat and add flavour. Available from Indian spice shops.

cassia bark Often mistakenly packaged and sold as cinnamon, dried cassia bark is thicker and harder than the related cinnamon bark. As it is a native of India, the best place to buy it is in an Indian spice shop.

chicken stock *see* page 164

chilli, chipotle Of Mexican origin, this is a jalapeno chilli that has been smoked during the drying process. It has a warming heat and a toasted, smoky flavour. Available dried or preserved in vinegar from specialty food shops.

coconut cream The thick cream scooped from the surface of first-pressed COCONUT MILK. This is the richest form of any coconut product. Available tinned or in block form from Asian food stores.

coconut milk Made by pressing the grated flesh of ripe coconuts that has been steeped in hot water. It is rich in oil and high in saturated fat. The first pressing gives the thickest milk; repeated pressings give a more diluted milk each time. Available tinned from Asian food stores. Choose a reliable brand, preferably Thai. The white milk should be unsweetened and have a smooth consistency.

coconut vinegar A mild vinegar with a low acidity level made from coconut water, the milky liquid that spills out when the coconut is cracked open. Two brands are available from Asian food stores. The Thai brand is a clear vinegar; the one from the Philippines has a milky appearance. Either type can be used.

dariole moulds *see* dessert moulds

date, black Of Chinese origin, this dried date has a dense, smoky taste. The seed must be removed before cooking. Available from Asian food stores.

demi-glace A reduced stock used in the preparation of sauces. Reduce BEEF or VEAL STOCK by half until it is thick and shiny and coats the back of a cold spoon. Do not over-reduce or you will end up with something that looks like Vegemite and is very salty. The stock sets to a jelly when cooled.

dessert moulds Some of the dessert recipes in this book call for particular moulds. The dariole moulds I refer to are 5 cm wide × 8 cm high, hold 200 ml each and are made of stainless steel or aluminium. Bavarois moulds are made of either stainless steel or plastic and are 6 cm wide × 5 cm high and hold 100 ml. Slight variations in size and volume are acceptable, but watch out for cooking times and the given yield.

dry-roast *see* instructions under spices, roasting and grinding

duck stock *see* page 164

egg wash Used for glazing pastry and breads and made by beating egg yolks with a fork in a bowl. Use a pastry brush for application.

eggplant, smoked To prepare, prick whole eggplants a few times with a skewer and sit over a barbecue grill or a direct flame until the skin blisters and blackens on all sides. When cool enough to handle, peel off the skin and squeeze out any bitter juices. The flesh will have a smoky flavour. Use while still warm for maximum flavour.

fish sauce Made from small fish that have been fermented in the sun with salt; a form of 'liquid salt' with more complexity and intensity of flavour than table or sea salt. I prefer to use the Thai 'Squid' brand as I find it is not too salty. The salt content of brands varies, so test each recipe if using a different brand; you may need to use less or more. Available from Asian food stores.

fish stock *see* page 165

ginger juice To prepare, cut 2 washed knobs of fresh ginger into a fine dice. Put into a food processor bowl with just enough cold water to wet the ginger. Process for 1–2 minutes, then press through a fine-mesh sieve or muslin to extract as much juice as possible. Store in the refrigerator. The ginger pulp can be used for flavouring a stock or sauce.

gluten flour Used to boost the gluten content of plain or 'soft' flour. It is not necessary to use gluten flour if using the harder bread flour. Higher gluten levels in bread and pasta doughs give greater elasticity and a better end result. Available from health-food stores.

jelly bag A necessary item to have on hand when preserving. Available from specialty shops and some supermarkets or you can improvise by using several layers of muslin cloth or oil-filter bags.

lime leaves, kaffir A staple ingredient in Thai cooking and available fresh, frozen or dried from Asian food stores. There is no substitute for the fresh leaves that are shredded in salads. Use frozen or dried leaves only if cooking; even then they won't impart the same citrus taste as the fresh leaves.

mirin A sweet Japanese cooking wine made from rice. Available from Asian food stores.

mitzuba A salad green or vegetable of Japanese origin known as trefoil, now grown in semi-tropical parts of Australia. The fragrant leaf can be eaten raw or very lightly steamed. Another salad green, such as MIZUNA, can be used instead if mitzuba is unavailable.

mizuna A salad green of Japanese origin that is becoming increasingly available. Sold in bunches, and often used in mesclun salad mix, it has long, fern-like leaves that taste quite mild and act as a good carrier for dressings.

nigella seeds Small black seeds similar in appearance to black onion seeds and often mistakenly referred to as black cummin. This spice comes from India and is featured widely in many spice blends. Available from Indian spice shops.

nori seaweed sheets Made from laver, a highly nutritious seaweed, and as thin as paper, these are used for making sushi. The greenish sheets have already been toasted, the black ones are untoasted. Toasting nori sheets improves their flavour and texture. To toast, hold a nori sheet with a pair of tongs over a direct flame for a few seconds. Available from Asian food stores. Once the packet has been opened, the sheets should be kept in a sealed, dry container as they deteriorate with moisture.

nuts, roasting and grinding *see* instructions under spices, roasting and grinding

onion, caramelised To prepare, slice brown onions finely and cook in a good quantity of oil in a wide-based frying pan over moderate heat until the onion turns a caramel colour and tastes sweet. Strain from the oil when cooked. Reserve the flavoured oil for other cooking.

passionfruit juice To prepare, remove passionfruit pulp with a spoon, then press the pulp through a fine-mesh sieve, squeezing out as much juice as possible. Discard the seeds. Freeze the juice for future use. Passionfruit juice is not available in instant form, so this process is necessary to achieve the intense flavour of the fruit without the presence of the seeds. It takes about 25 ripe passionfruit to make 250 ml juice.

pepper, sichuan A stock ingredient in Chinese cooking that comes from the prickly ash tree. The berries resemble peppercorns and impart a distinctive, mildly hot flavour.

prawn stock *see* page 165

prawns, dried In fact, small shrimp that have been dried. Reconstitute in warm water before using or DRY-ROAST and grind where required. Available from Asian food stores.

ras el hanout A North African mixture of dried herbs and spices blended by the head of the spice shop according to the region and particular fancies of the blender. It is not readily available in Australia. Refer to *North African Cookery* by Arto der Haroutunian and Jill Norman's *Complete Book of Spices* for a thorough explanation of the many ingredients needed to make the blend, as well as suggestions for its use. There really is no substitute for it, but you could use a mild, yellow, spicy curry powder in its place. This spice mixture is so wonderful and difficult to substitute that I am, in fact, considering importing it.

rice, arborio A variety of Italian rice, slightly starchy with big round grains, used specifically for making risotto. The two varieties available are superfini and semifini, the latter having smaller grains.

rice wine, brown Shaosing wine is a staple ingredient in Chinese cooking and is made from rice brewed with water. The closest substitute is dry sherry, although it won't give the same flavour. Available from Asian food stores.

saffron butter To prepare, heat 50 ml TOMATO ESSENCE until it boils and add 2 g saffron threads and infuse for a few minutes. Whip 250 g softened unsalted butter in a food processor and gradually pour in the saffron liquid until incorporated. Keep stored in a sealed container in the refrigerator. Stir into sauces at the last minute to enrich the flavour.

shallots, fried A deep-fried garnish made from red (Asian) shallots. To prepare, peel the shallots and slice finely lengthwise. Fry over a moderately high heat in quite a deep layer of vegetable oil until golden brown. Remove from the heat immediately, pour the hot oil through a sieve into a stainless steel bowl and spread the fried shallots onto paper towels to cool. Store in a sealed container to keep crisp. Also available ready-made from Asian food stores.

soy sauce, dark I use thick, black soy sauce rather than the thin varieties, and prefer the 'Elephant' brand, which tastes less salty than others and includes some sugar. There is no substitute – be careful never to buy cheap imitation brands. Available from Asian food stores.

spices, roasting and grinding Necessary to develop the oil, aroma and flavour of the spice to avoid it tasting 'raw'. To prepare, heat a cast-iron or heavy-based frying pan until hot and dry-roast (without oil) each spice separately. Toss the pan over a low heat until the spice is aromatic and darker in colour. Allow the spice to cool on a plate before grinding in a spice grinder or mortar and pestle. Once spices have been roasted and ground they are best used immediately as their flavour and intensity becomes weaker when stored. When buying spices, it is best to purchase them in small quantities whole and roast and grind them as you need them. Buy from a shop that does brisk trade, so you won't be buying anything too old.

squab stock *see* page 165

squid ink The fishy-tasting, black liquid from the 'ink' sacs of squid or cuttlefish used to colour pasta or noodles or impart flavour. To obtain, remove the ink sacs and squeeze the ink carefully into whatever you are adding. It is a messy and time-consuming process, but becomes easier and faster with experience. Squid ink is now available frozen; however, few places stock it and quantities suitable for domestic use are uncommon in Australia. Essential Ingredient, a food lover's mecca in Sydney, always has it on hand.

sterilising jars Sterilised jars are necessary for ensuring that preserves do not spoil or become contaminated. Heat kills bacteria and organisms that cause spoilage. To sterilise jars, wash them in boiling water or in a dishwasher and dry in a warm oven until ready for use. The hot food item is put into the hot, dry jars and sealed immediately.

stock *see* pages 164–65

sugar, palm A dense sugar made from the sap of the coconut palm. Available from Asian food stores in block or cake form; there is also a softer variety available in jars. I use a Thai brand – a flat round cake, pale gold in colour – that crumbles easily when cut with a sharp knife.

sugar, rock Less refined than white sugar and available in gold-coloured rock form. It has a mild sweetness and gives a slight glaze to the food with which it is cooked. It needs to be broken up with a mallet as it is quite solid. Don't attempt to use a knife. Available from Asian food stores.

sun-dried tomato paste Used for flavouring and made by blending chopped sun-dried tomatoes with olive oil to form a paste. Australian and imported brands of ready-made paste are available from selected food stores.

syrup, orange An intense syrup used to flavour desserts. To prepare, make a double-strength SUGAR SYRUP (twice as much sugar to water) and add the juice and zest of a few sweet oranges during the cooking. Cook until quite syrupy. Keeps indefinitely, refrigerated.

syrup, sugar Used in the preparation of desserts and made with equal quantities of castor sugar and water. To prepare, bring water to a boil and cook until the sugar has dissolved. 1 litre water and 1 kg sugar yields about 1.5 litres sugar syrup. Keeps indefinitely, refrigerated.

tahini A paste made from crushed sesame seeds commonly used in Lebanese and Middle Eastern cooking. Available from most food stores and supermarkets. Keep refrigerated once opened.

tamarind juice Used as a souring agent and obtained by soaking a block of tamarind pulp, a by-product of the pods of the tamarind tree. To prepare, soak the tamarind pulp in water, bring to a boil and simmer for 1 hour. Tamarind pulp is available from Asian or Indian food stores and some supermarkets.

tangerine peel, dried Used to add a citrus flavour to a wide variety of dishes. To reconstitute, soften in warm water, remove any unwanted pith and mince finely, if the recipe calls for it, or, if adding to a stock for flavouring, add in the whole piece. Available from Asian food stores. To make it yourself, take the peel from fresh tangerines and dry on a wire rack in a warm, dry place. Keep the dried peel in a sealed container.

tatsoi A small green leaf of Japanese origin that grows in clusters and requires very little cooking due to its size and fragility. Related to the Chinese flat cabbage. Usually available from Asian food stores in loose leaf form. Snow pea leaves or bok choy can be used instead if necessary.

tomato essence The liquid that is expelled when pulped ripe tomatoes are left to drain through muslin or a JELLY BAG suspended over a bucket. To keep the essence clear, do not push or force the pulp through the bag. 5 kg tomatoes will yield about 1 litre of essence over a 24-hour period. To make reduced tomato essence, bring the essence to a boil and reduce by half to increase the sweetness slightly and intensify the flavour.

tomato purée Not to be confused with tomato paste, which is thicker and stronger tasting. To prepare, purée chopped ripe tomatoes in a food processor, sieve out the seeds and cook over a low heat for 2 hours until slightly thickened. Keep refrigerated. Also available from supermarkets.

tomatoes, oven-dried To prepare, cut ripe and perfect roma tomatoes in half lengthwise. Arrange on a baking tray cut-side up and sprinkle with a little sea salt and castor sugar. Place the tray in an oven set on 50°C and leave until the tomatoes begin to dry out but still remain quite soft. Best done overnight when the oven is not needed, the process takes 15–20 hours, depending on the moisture content of the tomatoes. Check at regular intervals. Store in a jar, cover with virgin olive oil and spike with a couple of whole garlic cloves, a few basil leaves and some pepper. Keeps for 3 months, refrigerated.

tomatoes, roasting A method of cooking tomatoes whole to soften them and bring out their sweetness before using them in a particular recipe. To prepare, arrange ripe tomatoes in a single layer in a lightly oiled roasting pan and roast in a hot oven for 30 minutes until coloured and soft.

Vietnamese mint A hot-tasting, aromatic mint with long, pointed green leaves with purple markings that is a staple ingredient of Vietnamese cooking. It grows prolifically, especially in warmer humid climates, and constant pruning activates growth. Sprout in water until the stalks strike roots, and plant. Available from Asian food stores, where it is often sold as *rau ram*.

vine leaves Preserved grape vine leaves in brine used to package other food items, particularly in Greek and Middle Eastern cooking. Wash the leaves in cold water to remove any unwanted salty flavour. Available from all food stores.

water chestnut A crunchy sweet vegetable of Chinese origin with a black outer layer that peels away easily with a knife to reveal a white disc with a firm texture. Available fresh for a short time in spring or tinned from Asian food stores and most supermarkets. They can be eaten raw or cooked and keep for 2 weeks in the refrigerator when fresh. Rinse tinned water chestnuts under cold water and blanch briefly in boiling water before use.

STOCK

beef/veal stock

A rich stock made from roasted beef bones, shanks and veal shins that forms the basis of good sauces and soups. Keeps for 4 days, refrigerated.

2 kg beef bones
2 kg shanks, split
2 kg veal knuckles (osso bucco)
1 litre red wine
10 ripe tomatoes
4 brown onions, chopped
2 large carrots, chopped
handful of parsley (including stalks)
1 tablespoon black peppercorns
2 sprigs of thyme

1 Brown the bones in a roasting pan in a hot oven, then put them in a stockpot large enough to hold them with room to spare.

2 Remove any fat from the roasting pan. Deglaze the pan with the wine and add the wine to the stockpot.

3 Roast the tomatoes, onion and carrot in the roasting pan until softened and add to the stockpot. Add the remaining ingredients and cover with cold water. Bring the stockpot to a boil, then reduce the heat and gently simmer for 6 hours. Skim the surface regularly with a mesh spoon to remove any scum.

4 Remove the stockpot from the heat, carefully take out the bones with tongs and pass the stock through a conical sieve and then through a fine-mesh sieve to remove any sediment. Ladle off any fat. Allow to cool completely before refrigerating. Remove any fat from the chilled stock before using or freezing.

chicken stock

A white stock made from chicken bones and meat and used in a multitude of preparations. Keeps for 4 days, refrigerated.

2 chicken carcasses, broken up or 1 kg bones
1 chicken
several slices fresh ginger
handful of spring onion tops
1 tablespoon white peppercorns
500 ml white wine

1 Wash the chicken bones in cold water to remove any blood.

2 Put the bones and whole chicken in a stockpot with remaining ingredients. Cover the bones with cold water.

3 Bring the stockpot to a boil over a gentle heat and simmer slowly for 2 hours. Skim the surface regularly with a mesh spoon to remove any scum.

4 Remove the solids carefully and strip the meat from the chicken and keep for another use. Pass the stock through a fine-mesh sieve to remove any sediment. Allow to cool completely before refrigerating. Remove any fat from the chilled stock before using or freezing.

duck stock

Make this when you have used the duck meat for another purpose, as the bones will still have a lot of flavour. It is a good stock base to have on hand for making soup or a sauce and necessary when making Five-spice Duck and Shiitake Mushroom Pies (see page 98). Keeps for 4 days, refrigerated.

4 duck carcasses, broken up
2 brown onions, chopped
1 head of garlic, cut in half
5 spring onions, chopped
1 knob fresh ginger, sliced
a little vegetable oil
2 bay leaves
1 teaspoon black peppercorns
handful of parsley
5 litres CHICKEN STOCK

1 Brown the duck carcasses in a hot oven to render some of their fat.

2 In a large stockpot, sauté the onion, garlic, spring onion and ginger in a little oil until fragrant. Add the bay leaves, peppercorns and parsley and stir. Add the browned duck bones and cover with the chicken stock.

3 Bring the stockpot to a boil, then simmer gently for 3 hours, uncovered. Skim the surface regularly with a mesh spoon to remove any fat and scum.

4 Pass the stock through a conical sieve, pressing firmly on the bones to extract as much juice and flavour as possible. Discard the solids. Pass the stock through a fine-mesh sieve, allow it to settle and remove any fat that comes to the surface as it cools. Allow to cool completely before refrigerating. Remove any fat from the chilled stock before using or freezing.

fish stock

A good stock to have handy as it forms the basis for many soups and sauces. Use good quality, fresh, cleaned fish heads and bones for the best flavour. Keeps for 3 days, refrigerated.

heads and bones of 2 large fish (preferably snapper)
6 spring onions, chopped
1 knob fresh ginger, sliced
1 teaspoon white peppercorns
500 ml white wine

1 Wash the fish heads thoroughly to remove any blood. Make sure the gills have been removed as they will give the stock a sour flavour if left on.

2 Place all the ingredients in a stockpot and cover with cold water. Bring to a boil, then simmer gently for 2 hours. Skim the surface regularly with a mesh spoon to remove any scum.

3 Pass the stock through a conical sieve, pressing the bones to extract as much juice as possible. Discard the solids. Pass the stock through a fine-mesh sieve or muslin to remove any sediment. Allow to cool completely before refrigerating.

prawn stock

Use the heads and shells from fresh green prawns to make this rich, fragrant stock. Once cooled after cooking, it is best kept frozen.

6 tomatoes
1 kg green prawn heads and shells
100 ml Chinese brown rice wine (shaosing)
50 ml vegetable oil
1 brown onion, chopped
6 cloves garlic, sliced
3 slices fresh ginger
2 slices galangal
1 stalk lemongrass, finely sliced
2 red bird's-eye chillies, chopped
1 teaspoon sichuan peppercorns
1 teaspoon fennel seeds
1 star anise
2 kaffir lime leaves, chopped
3 litres FISH STOCK

1 Roast the tomatoes in a hot oven until softened and set aside.

2 Heat a large wok and toss the prawn heads and shells until they start to colour, then add the rice wine and deglaze. Remove from the heat.

3 In a stockpot, heat the oil and sauté the remaining ingredients until they start to colour and become aromatic. Add the cooked prawn heads and their juices, the tomatoes and the fish stock. Bring the stock to a boil and simmer gently for 2 hours. Skim the surface regularly with a mesh spoon to remove any scum. Pass the stock through a conical sieve, pressing to extract as much juice as possible. Discard the solids.

4 Pass the stock through a fine-mesh sieve or muslin to remove any sediment. Allow to cool completely before freezing.

squab stock

A base stock to make when you have a supply of carcasses. Once made and cooled it keeps for 3 days, refrigerated.

10 squab or pigeon carcasses
2 brown onions, chopped
2 leeks, cleaned and sliced
6 large cloves garlic, sliced
1 carrot, sliced
a little vegetable oil
2 sprigs of thyme
handful of parsley
2 teaspoons black peppercorns
2 bay leaves
300 ml red wine
2 litres CHICKEN STOCK

1 Brown the carcasses in a roasting pan in a hot oven. Drain off any fat.

2 Heat a large stockpot and sauté the onion, leeks, garlic and carrot in a little oil until softened.

3 Add the thyme, parsley, peppercorns and bay leaves and stir for a minute or two. Add the wine and allow to boil for a few minutes. Add the chicken stock, bring to a boil and simmer for 3 hours. Skim the surface with a mesh spoon regularly to remove any fat and scum.

4 Pass the stock through a conical sieve, pressing the bones to extract as much juice as possible. Discard the solids. Pass the stock through a fine-mesh sieve or muslin to remove any sediment. Skim any excess fat from the surface with a ladle. Allow to cool completely before refrigerating. Remove any fat from the chilled stock before using or freezing.

Index